ANTHONY MATTINA

IRREGULARITY in SYNTAX

TRANSATLANTIC SERIES in LINGUISTICS
Under the general editorship of
Samuel R. Levin
Hunter College
of the City University
of New York

ANALYTIC SYNTAX

OTTO JESPERSEN

THE STUDY OF SYNTAX

The Generative-Transformational Approach
to the Structure of American English

D. TERENCE LANGENDOEN

INTRODUCTION TO TAGMEMIC ANALYSIS

WALTER A. COOK, S.J.

IRREGULARITY in SYNTAX

GEORGE LAKOFF

The University of Michigan

HOLT, RINEHART AND WINSTON, INC.

New York Chicago San Francisco Atlanta
Dallas Montreal Toronto London Sydney

To my parents,
Herman and Ida Lakoff

Foreword

The appearance of this volume marks the end of the long period during which George Lakoff's *On the Nature of Syntactic Irregularity* (henceforth, *ONSI*) has been an underground classic, circulated in the form of a Harvard Computation Laboratory progress report and countless second and third order Xeroxes of that report, and quoted in scholarly journals more often than all but a handful of aboveground linguistics books have been.

There are three principal reasons for the unusual interest that *ONSI* aroused shortly after its semipublication. First, Lakoff presented in it a large body of analyses that the theory of Noam Chomsky's *Aspects of the Theory of Syntax* allowed, which could be justified on the basis of the same kinds of arguments that had hitherto been given in support of specific transformational analyses, and that yielded deep structures considerably more semantically transparent than those hitherto proposed. Secondly, he took seriously the important conclusion (which has since been rejected by Chomsky) of Chomsky's *Aspects* that the meaning of a sentence be recoverable from its deep structure, and used semantic facts as evidence on a par with grammaticality judgments (rather than as something that one only looks at after he has decided what his syntactic analysis will be, as had been the current practice) in choosing between alternative syntactic analyses. Third, he cast great light on the concept of "grammatical category" by showing that the great profusion of category labels that had appeared in previous transformational work could be avoided and the inventory of categories reduced to a set that could lay some claim to universality; indeed, the way in which Lakoff's theory of exceptions affects the notion of "grammatical category" is the principal reason why what he in his preface says "was begun as a minor revision and extension of the conception of grammar presented in Chomsky's *Aspects of the Theory of Syntax*" not only "raise[d] some rather deep questions" but eventually led to drastic revisions in the foundations of grammatical theory.

Some other noteworthy things about *ONSI* that did not cause so much of a stir at the time it appeared but in my opinion have proved of at least as great importance in the subsequent development of grammatical theory are: (1) The use of the relative grammaticality of some ungrammatical sentences over others as evidence for grammatical analyses;[1] this type of argument has been put

---

[1]The Postal-Lakoff notion of relative grammaticality, while reminiscent of Chomsky's notion of "degree of grammaticality," is not equivalent to it, since it does not commit one to the position that any two sentences can be compared in degree of grammaticality and does not accord any special status to "fully grammatical" sentences.

to especially good use by Paul Postal in such works as *Cross-Over Phenomena* (another underground classic to be published as the next volume of the Transatlantic Series in Linguistics). (2) Lakoff's insistence that a generalization be incorporated into a grammar as a unit and his concomitant avoidance of the ubiquitous curly brackets of other transformational grammarians;[2] in this connection, see the explicit statements of note R F–2 and the implicit premise of Appendix A that if the rules discussed there contained the term {V, Adj}, they would fail to express the appropriate generalizations.[3] (3) The proposals of Chapter 9 that certain types of lexical item are syntactically complex, for example, that a clause with the verb *enter* is the inchoative of a clause with a verb of location.

The main reason why such analyses could not be developed very far in 1965 was the almost universal assumption that the insertion of lexical items had to precede all transformations. The acceptance of this assumption, incidentally, forced Lakoff to propose analyses that violated the "lexical base hypothesis" of Chapter 10, for example, the analysis of *enter* as a verb synonymous with *in* but obligatorily combined with the inchoative pro-verb by the inchoative transformation: according to this analysis, *enter* and *in* are synonymous items that not only do not "have the same deep structure distribution" but indeed are in complementary distribution in deep structure. The rejection of the claim that lexical insertion precedes all transformations (that is, the rejection of a level of "deep structure" in the sense of *Aspects*) allows one to say that ⟨ BECOME ⟩ (or whatever the basic inchoative element is called) is part of the meaning of *enter* and still have clauses with *enter* derived through an application of the inchoative transformation, or rather, the more general transformation of "predicate raising," of which "inchoative" and "causative" are special cases; this transformation combines the predicate element of one clause with that of the next higher clause and is involved in the derivation of not only inchoative and causative verbs but also such verbs as *look for* (= try to find), *malinger* (= pretend to be sick), and *forget* (= cease to know).[4]

---

[2] In a recent work, Lakoff has characterized curly brackets as "a formal device for expressing the claim that a generalization does not exist."

[3] The only real defect in the argument of Appendix A is that it lists the properties shared by verbs and adjectives without also enumerating in full and accounting for the differences between verbs and adjectives. However, to my knowledge, besides the two differences mentioned by Lakoff (adjectives but not verbs take a copula when used in predicate position; adjectives do not allow preposition deletion but verbs do), the only syntactic (as opposed to morphological) difference between verbs and adjectives is the position and form of adverbs of degree:

John is very fond of Susan.

John likes Susan very much.

[4] By the same token, the various nominalization transformations referred to in *ONSI* are special cases of a single prelexical nominalization transformation, which raises the predi-

Since the appearance of *ONSI*, transformational grammar has split into two principal lines of development for which I think it is worthwhile to give some bibliographical references here. The one line, which continues the general approach of *ONSI*, involves the rejection of a distinction between syntax and semantics (and thus of a level of "deep structure" as distinct from semantic representation), the replacement of the base component of *Aspects* by two systems of generative[5] rules: one defining the class of possible semantic representations and the other ("output constraints") restricting the class of possible surface structures, and detailed investigation of semantic representation. It is illustrated by the following works:

Emmon Bach, "Nouns and Noun Phrases." Bach and Harms (eds.), *Universals in Linguistic Theory* (New York: Holt, Rinehart and Winston, 1968), pp. 91–122.

Robert Binnick, Alice Davison, Georgia Green, and Jerry L. Morgan (eds.), *Papers from the Fifth Regional Meeting, Chicago Linguistic Society* (University of Chicago, 1969), especially the papers by Morgan, G. Lakoff, R. Lakoff, Ross, Postal, Lindholm, and Karttunen.

George Lakoff, *Generative Semantics* (New York: Holt, Rinehart and Winston, to appear in 1972).

D. T. Langendoen and Charles Fillmore (eds.), *Proceedings of the 1969 Ohio State Semantics Conference* (New York: Holt, Rinehart and Winston, in preparation).

James D. McCawley, "The Role of Semantics in a Grammar," Bach and Harms (eds.), *Universals in Linguistic Theory*, pp. 124–169.

---

cate element out of a relative clause and combines it with an element indicating what was relativized over, for example:

the inventor of the zilchtron
= the x such that x invent the zilchtron.

Schwartz's invention
= the x such that Schwartz invent x.

the invention by Schwartz of the zilchtron
= the x such that Schwartz invent $_x$ the zilchtron.

Here a subscript on a verb indicates the event being referred to. The embedded clauses are unspecified as to tense since there are sentences such as *Inventors of useful devices always have received and always will receive insufficient remuneration* whose derivations require that a nominalization that, if every underlying clause had to have a tense, would be derived from a structure containing 'x has invented a useful device' count as identical to one containing 'x will invent a useful device'. This fact, incidentally, provides evidence that the obligatoriness of tense in English corresponds to an output constraint rather than to a constraint on underlying structures.

[5]I will describe rules as "generative" if they specify what is possible or impossible at one specific stage of a derivation and "interpretive" if they specify how two stages of a derivation may or must differ. It is in this sense of "generative" that it makes sense to refer to this version of transformational grammar as involving "generative semantics." This distinction between "generative" and "interpretive" presupposes that a grammar is a set of constraints on allowable derivations; it would make no sense in conjunction with, for example, a conception of a grammar as a Turing machine. It is related but not identical to the distinction that Chomsky draws in *Aspects* (pp. 136, 143) between "creative" and "interpretive": Chomsky admits as "deep structures" only those structures generated by his base component that can form part of a complete derivation, and he calls "interpretive" those parts of the grammar that do not affect the class of deep structures (as rules that can cause a derivation to "block" might).

James D. McCawley, "Lexical Insertion in a Transformational Grammar without Deep Structure." C. J. Bailey, Bill J. Darden, and Alice Davison (eds.), *Papers from the Fourth Regional Meeting, Chicago Linguistic Society* (University of Chicago, 1968), pp. 71–80.

James D. McCawley, "English as a *VSO* Language." *Language,* March 1970.

Paul M. Postal, "On Coreferential Complement Subject Deletion." To appear in Steinberg and Jakobovitz (eds.), *Semantics: An Interdisciplinary Reader* (Cambridge University Press, 1971).

John Robert Ross, "Auxiliaries as Main Verbs." William Todd (ed.), *Studies in Philosophical Linguistics, Series One* (Evanston, Ill.: Great Expectations, 1969), pp. 77–102.

The other principal line of development, which is to some extent a reaction to the conclusions of the first line, rejects the principle that deep structure determines meaning, makes no explicit proposal as to the nature of semantic representation (the possibility of such a level of representation is doubted by at least some supporters of this approach), makes use of a highly language-specific base component generating deep structures that are relatively close to surface structure, and does not derive most "derived" words from deep structures involving the "basic" word but attempts to account for a derivational relation through a complex dictionary entry that indicates what properties are shared by the "basic" word and its derivatives. This approach is illustrated by the following works:

Noam A. Chomsky, "Remarks on Nominalization." To appear in Jacobs and Rosenbaum (eds.), *Readings in English Transformational Grammar* (Waltham, Mass.: Blaisdell, 1970).

Noam A. Chomsky, "Deep Structure, Surface Structure, and Semantic Interpretation." To appear in a *festschrift* for Shiro Hattori, and in Steinberg and Jakobovitz, *Semantics: An Interdisciplinary Reader* (Cambridge University Press, 1971).

Joseph E. Emonds, "A Structure-Preserving Constraint on NP Movement Transformations." Binnick et al., *Papers from the Fifth Regional Meeting, Chicago Linguistic Society,* pp. 60–65.

Ray S. Jackendoff, "An Interpretive Theory of Negation." *Foundations of Language,* 5:218–241 (1969).

Both of these lines of development are also represented by a large number of unpublished papers and dissertations. The importance of *ONSI* in the development of grammatical theory is made clear by the extent to which the issues that the works in both these bibliographies treat were first raised in *ONSI*.

Göteborg, Sweden   JAMES D. MCCAWLEY
September 1969

Preface

This book, my Indiana dissertation, was completed in the fall of 1965, and first appeared in December of that year as a National Science Foundation report under the title *On the Nature of Syntactic Irregularity*. It was begun as a minor revision and extension of the conception of grammar presented in Noam Chomsky's *Aspects of the Theory of Syntax*. Before the work was completed, it had become apparent that the revision was anything but minor. I began by trying to define the notion "exception to a transformational rule," which was a fairly tame enterprise. I noticed along the way that the proposed exception mechanism, which this work attempts to motivate on independent grounds, would (1) allow certain sentences to be derived from underlying structures that more closely reflected their semantic representations; (2) permit one to reformulate transformational rules by removing idiosyncratic restrictions, thus permitting transformations in one language to resemble more closely transformations in other languages; and (3) permit the base rules to be simplified, seemingly in the direction of providing universal base rules. Rather than being a trifling technical revision, the book turned out, almost surprisingly, to raise some rather deep questions.

I had originally planned to revise this work for formal publication, but advances in the field during 1966 made revision hopeless. Since it was out-of-date, I had resolved not to publish it. However, a number of students and colleagues have prevailed upon me to permit its publication, even in unrevised form. I do so with some reservations, and it is only fair that the reader should receive some indication of where I think the book goes wrong. Since this was meant to be a conservative work in transformational grammar, I assumed the general framework of Chomsky's *Aspects of the Theory of Syntax,* including his notion of "deep structure," which assumed that all lexical items were inserted before any transformations applied. This assumption has since been proved false, and another alternative was available even at that time. During the summer of 1965, Jeff Gruber had suggested to me that irregular nominals like *aggression* could be handled by assuming that lexical insertion was posttransformational, and that transformations operated on abstract structures containing indications of meaning, but no lexical items. In retrospect, it seems clear that Gruber was right, and that many examples that I handled by the use of absolute exceptions should have been handled by a lexical specification of posttransformational structure. Most of the other examples of absolute exceptions can be eliminated on other grounds. D. M. Perlmutter has argued persuasively that cases like *attempt* and *implore* should be treated not as absolute exceptions to equi-NP-deletion, but as words that respectively require and forbid their subjects and the subjects of their complements to be coreferential in underlying structure. This possibility was also open to me at the time the book was written; Paul Postal had suggested it as a possible alternative. I rejected it because of its inability to handle cases like **I attempted for Max to be slugged by me*, where the Perlmutter constraint on underlying structures would be met, but the sentence would nonetheless be ungrammatical. However, it has since been discovered that such sentences are unrelated to the equi-subject constraint, since non-equi-subject verbs like *want* are also ruled out in such cases: **I wanted for Max to be slugged by me*. I would accept Perlmutter's criticism, as well as Gruber's. Although I think that absolute exceptions were a mistake, it seems to me that they were necessary, given the greater error of assuming the existence of a level of deep structure. Hypothetical lexical items were also a necessity, given the assumption that lexical insertion was pretransformational. In retrospect, hypothetical lexical items should be looked upon as a way of coding posttransformational structures and global constraints into lexical items. Given posttransformational lexical insertion and global constraints on lexical insertion rules, hypothetical lexical items can be eliminated and transformations can be conceived of as operating on phrase markers containing atomic predicates. Boolean exceptions can now be looked upon as codings of global constraints on derivations.

Very little is said here concerning the important phenomenon of rule government. John Ross and I have observed that relatively few rules can have lexical exceptions. Rules containing essential variables and rules that move verbs cannot have lexical exceptions. Rules whose domain of application is a clause and its immediately embedded complement clause seem always to be capable of having exceptions (for example, equi-NP-deletion, subject-raising, negative-transportation, complementizer-placement). In percentages, the proportion of rules that may have lexical exceptions seems, according to our present knowledge, to be very small, perhaps as few as one in ten. Thus, it would seem that, once the general principles of rule government are worked out, the descriptive power of the theory of exceptions would be drastically limited.

The discerning reader will observe that the level of argumentation in this work, though normal for 1965, is appallingly low by contemporary standards. The reason is simple enough. In 1965, so little work had been done in transformational grammar that analyses were rarely in conflict, and no alternative theories had been seriously proposed. That situation changed radically within a year, in part because of the reaction of some linguists to the analyses proposed in this work. On the whole, I would say that detailed investigation in the past five years has borne out the correctness of many of the analyses presented here, though they were originally proposed on the basis of slim evidence. These results however, have, not been universally accepted, largely because the foundations of the field have been brought into question, in reaction, in part, to this work. To the extent that it has raised interesting questions, it has served its purpose.

GEORGE LAKOFF

Ann Arbor, Michigan
July 1970

Introduction

Generative grammar starts from the premise that a natural language is based on a system of rules. The premise is necessary since languages are infinite, and it is only in terms of rules that apply recursively that we can produce and understand the new sentences that we utter and hear every day. Within the past ten years, studies in generative grammar have made it clear that many such rules must take the form of grammatical transformations, although the exact nature of transformations remains an open question.

Originally, it was thought that all syntactic rules, including grammatical transformations were "regular"—that their applicability was determined solely by the occurrence of natural grammatical categories. In such a system, "irregularities" were impossible, and any apparent irregularities were assumed to reflect the existence of hitherto undiscovered natural grammatical categories. Recent attempts to account for apparent irregularities, however, have resulted in the postulation of a large number of grammatical categories that are anything but "natural." A great many of them have had to be postulated only to account for the peculiarities of individual lexical items in their interactions with isolated rules in a single language. These results suggest that the original assumption was wrong and that irregularities are a normal part of language.

Such facts have led Paul Postal to initiate a conception of grammar in which lexical irregularities not only are possible, but play a large role. Postal's notion of grammar incorporates the following constraints: (1) transformations may not mention individual lexical items; (2) the possible irregularities in a language are in some way defined by the set of rules in the grammar itself; (3) grammatical morphemes may not appear segmentally in deep structures, that is, the terminal elements of deep structures may only be lexical items; and (4) there are only two categories of lexical items: *nouns* and what we will call VERBS (a category containing what have traditionally been called adjectives and verbs).

This study is an exploration into Postal's conception of grammar. It is an attempt to define the notion "possible irregularity" in a natural language. The contributions that the present work makes to this conception of grammar are the notions of (1) rule government, (2) minor rules, (3) absolute exceptions characterized by structural description features, (4) Boolean exceptions, and (5) the lexical base.

For the sake of coherence, we have excluded from the main body of the text some lengthy discussions of our background assumptions and of questions of peripheral interest. These appear in a series of appendixes at the end of the volume. The appendixes are, for the most part, self-contained and may be read independently of the bulk of the text.

I have been very fortunate in having had provocative teachers and colleagues and I would like to express my gratitude to them. None of the work in this volume would have been possible without the guidance of Paul Postal. He first pointed out to me the problems surrounding irregularities and gave unsparingly of his time to discuss these problems with me and to work over the original manuscript. During my stay in Indiana, Fred W. Householder was a constant source of stimulating discussion. He has read the manuscript and provided many valuable criticisms. My first linguistics teachers, Noam Chomsky and Morris Halle, fired my interest in the subject and have been helpful in many ways since my undergraduate days. Bruce Fraser, Jay Keyser, Edward Klima, Lester Rice, John R. Ross, and Susumu Kuno read the manuscript and provided comments and criticisms that resulted in a number of changes. I am also indebted to Louis Gross, James D. McCawley, and Peter Rosenbaum for enlightening discussions of many of the topics covered here. None of these people are in any way accountable for my mistakes.

Many of the most insightful suggestions that I have incorporated into this work have come from my wife, Robin T. Lakoff. Her keen insight into the workings of language has kept me from falling into error many times, and she has provided many of the crucial examples on which my arguments hinge. I doubt that this work could have been completed without her patience and encouragement.

I would also like to thank the U.S. Office of Education and the American Council of Learned Societies for fellowships under which much of this work was done. This book was completed while I was working at the Computation Laboratory at Harvard University, under National Science Foundation Grant GN-329 to Harvard University.

G. L.

Cambridge, Massachusetts
October 1965

Contents

1 GRAMMARS AND THE THEORY OF GRAMMAR

We take the province of linguistic theory to be defined by the following questions: What distinguishes natural languages from all other conceivable sets of objects? What do they have in common and in what ways can they possibly differ? To ask such questions is simply to ask for a precise characterization of what a natural language is (and, correspondingly, what it is not).

1.1 ADULT LANGUAGE LEARNING

When an adult learns a new language, he approaches it with certain preconceptions—exclusive of the idiosyncracies of his native language. He knows something of what to expect. He knows that the set of sentences in that language will differ markedly from the set of possible differential equations, the set of sequences of real numbers, the set of possible checker games, and an indefinitely large number of other sets. Although the sentences of the language will be unfamiliar to him, he can expect that they will be related to things that are quite familiar to him, namely, meanings. He knows in advance that he will be called upon to produce and recognize sequences of individual sounds that can be produced by the human vocal tract, and he will be expected to relate these sound sequences to meanings.

Before he starts, he knows that no matter what language he is involved with, he will be called upon to learn individual lexical items, that is, to pair isolated meanings with instructions as to how to pronounce the sequences of sounds that represent them. He can count on being able to form simple sentences from individual items by placing them one after another in some order. In fact, he begins with some notion of what a simple sentence is, and even more remarkable, he knows that he will be able in some sense to form complicated sentences from simple ones, though, of course, it will not be obvious to

1

him how to do so. And he can be certain that the arbitrary natural language he has chosen to learn will have conjunction; it will have nouns; it will have ways of speaking about certain basic human activities; and it will have ways of stating assertions, asking questions, and ordering people to do things. These are but a few of the things that each of us knows about any given human language—simply by virtue of our being human and its being a language. We are asking exactly what this knowledge is.

1.2 CHILD LANGUAGE LEARNING

Such knowledge is, of course, not confined to adults. A child raised in China will speak Chinese; one brought up in Finland will speak Finnish. Children seem to be able to learn any arbitrary natural language. It seems unlikely that they would be able to do so if they did not have some innate ability to learn natural languages. To ask what this ability is seems to be equivalent to asking what all natural languages share.

Consider the remarkable feat that each normal child performs in learning his native language. Having been exposed to a small number of utterances, the child begins to compose his own new utterances. At a very early stage, these new utterances cannot be considered random babblings or attempts at repetition. Rather, it appears as if the child has constructed a theory of what a correct utterance is, and he attempts to use that theory to communicate intelligently. When his theory is incorrect and he utters ungrammatical sentences, his elders correct him and he revises his theory. In a very short time, by the time the child is three or four, he has composed a theory that is very nearly correct, and can speak his native language fluently. That is, from that time on, he can understand altogether new sentences of his language, which he has never heard before, and in response, he can utter appropriate grammatical sentences, almost all of which are entirely new to him and most of which, in all probability, have never been uttered before in the history of the human race.

Each of us possesses this remarkable ability, and each of us has performed such a feat of theory construction. We are asking what are the principles, which we evidently all share, on which we have based these theories. Clearly such principles must exist. There are an infinite number of formal systems to serve as possible theories of some subject matter or other, just as there is an infinite range of subject matter to theorize about. It can safely be assumed that a child, confronted by the strange continuous sound signals emanating from his parents, does not start from scratch choosing random subject matter to theorize about and looking at randomly chosen theories to see if they fit whatever subject matter he has chosen. If this were so, a child would be just as likely to come up with a theory of physical acoustics as with a theory of how natural languages work in general and how his native language works in particular. Certainly a theory of natural language is at least as abstract and sophisticated as a theory of acoustics; indeed, it is so sophisticated that scholars working over the centuries have not been able to specify exactly what a natural language can be. Yet somehow each child, regardless of intelligence, knows this and uses this knowledge to construct a grammar of his own language.

To ask what are the principles by which we have constructed the grammars of the natural languages we know seems to be equivalent to asking what a natural language is, or what characterizes the grammars of all possible natural languages.

1.3 LINGUISTIC THEORY

One can conceive of the problem in other ways, of course. Imagine an abstract automaton that could generate all possible grammars of all possible natural languages and only these. Think of it as a mechanical procedure, which if followed will lead to the construction of all and only the possible grammars of possible natural languages. Such a mechanical procedure would be one way of characterizing what a natural language is. Of course, it need not be thought of as a mechanical procedure at all, but only as a set of conditions that all grammars of natural languages must meet. We will call such an autotomaton a "theory of grammar," a "theory of language," and a "linguistic theory." If grammars are considered as theories of particular natural languages, such automata may be considered as metatheories. We will refer to rules of such metatheories as "metarules" or "universal rules."

In practical terms a tentative metatheory constructed by linguists may fail in at least two ways. (1) It may fail to characterize an adequate grammar of some existing natural language. That is, it may in principle be unable to account for one or more phenomena in a single natural language. (2) It may characterize objects that could not be grammars of natural languages. For instance, our theory may allow for the expression of rules or combinations of rules that do not, and presumably, could not occur in any language. If inadequacy (1) arises, we must broaden our metatheory to include grammars that could describe the phenomena in question adequately, but not lose the ability to describe what it already can describe. If inadequacy (2) arises, we will have to constrain our metatheory to eliminate the objects that cannot be adequate grammars for some language, while not eliminating any that can.

Of course, in practice no linguist can ever be sure that he is working with an accurate, consistent, and fully specified metatheory. Rather, in actual practice, linguists attempt to expand or limit the scope of such metatheories on the basis of empirical evidence. In this study, we will be doing both. First, we shall point out that current theories of grammar cannot handle many kinds of syntactic irregularities and we shall propose an expanded metatheory that will do so. We will argue this primarily on the basis of evidence from English. Secondly, we will observe that the expanded metatheory can be constrained in certain ways, apparently without sacrificing its ability to characterize real languages.

1.4 THE FORM OF A LINGUISTIC THEORY

In recent years there has been a great deal of discussion of the goals of linguistic theory, or of what the automaton described in Section 1.3 should be capable of doing. We assume that the goals described by Chomsky [1965b, Chapter 1] are reasonable ones and define an interesting area of study. Attempts at justifying these goals have also been made in the following works: Chomsky, 1955, 1957, 1962b, 1964, 1965a and c; and Postal 1964a and b. By way of justifying our interests, we have nothing to add to what has already been said in these works.

However, since this study is meant as a contribution to the theory of language, that is, a proposal about what the automaton above should look like, perhaps we should reiterate and try to clarify those assumptions about linguistic theory that we will lean on most heavily.

In Section 1.3, we set ourselves the task of constructing an automaton that would in turn construct possible grammars of possible natural languages. We can view this task as having three closely related parts: (1) providing a universal vocabulary, the elements of which will be used to construct grammars; (2) defining the form of rules to be used in these grammars; (3) providing an organization of a possible grammar, that is, setting up components of a grammar that contain certain types of rules that use certain types of vocabulary elements, and stating the way in which these components may be related.

1.41 Vocabulary

A linguistic theory will have to contain a vocabulary of units from which grammars can be constructed. For instance, the units on the phonological level might be distinctive features such as those defined by Jakobson. On the syntactive level, they might be category symbols, such as S, NP, VP, N, V, and so on, and syntactic features, such as [+ANIMATE] or [−ABSTRACT]. Many students of language have observed that all languages seem to have nouns and verbs, vowels and consonants, and seem to share other elements as well. Thus, it seems that some of these elements will function in the grammars of all natural languages. This is, of course, an empirical question, but our best guess right now is that there are many such units.

Other units seem to function in a wide variety of languages, but not in all. For instance, most languages have passives, but a few do not. A large number of languages have articles, but by no means all. And so on. A major desideratum of a universal vocabulary is that all units should occur either in all languages, or in a wide variety of languages. A unit that appears in only one language, and plays a minor role in that language, will be a suspicious candidate for such a vocabulary.

Since any unit that occurs in the grammar of any natural language will have to appear in such a vocabulary, we might ask whether linguists have had to postulate units that seem to occur only in one particular language and that cannot be explained away as wrong analyses. The answer is that they have, in particular, in cases of irregularity. [For example, see Section 3.1.] As we shall see later, these seem to be spurious units, since they serve only to indicate that isolated lexical items must or must not undergo some rule or some combination of rules. One of the results of this study will be to show that we can eliminate these units from the universal vocabulary. Instead, we shall revise our tentative linguistic theory so that, given the rules of a grammar, our theory will automatically define, *in terms of that grammar,* the set of features that can possibly function to distinguish irregularities in the language generated by it.

1.42 The Types of Rules

Since natural languages exhibit an enormously wide variety of phenomena, one might guess that an equally wide variety of kinds of rules would be necessary to describe these phenomena. But this is not the case. As it turns out, the types of rules actually needed to form grammars of natural languages are very few in number and are of a very restricted sort. One of the major problems of the linguistic theorist is to figure out exactly what kinds of rules are necessary and what kinds are not.

Perhaps the best way to consider the nature of the problem is to ask what kinds of rules we can rule out a priori, simply by employing our intuitions as to what a language can be like. Let us look at some logically possible rules, which we know in advance could not occur in a natural language and which, indeed, have never been found to occur in any.

1. It is logically possible that in some natural language, imperative sentences could be the mirror images of their corresponding declarative sentences (that is, declarative sentences spoken backwards).
2. It is logically possible that a natural language could exist in which the number of nouns in each sentence always had to be equal to the cube of the number of prepositions.
3. It is logically possible that a natural language could exist in

which each sentence had to contain exactly a prime number of words.

4. It is logically possible that in some natural language the $5x$th word has to be identical to the $5x+1$th word, for all x.

No natural language like any of these has ever been found, and we know in advance that none ever will be found simply because we know that natural languages do not work like that. Therefore, we know in advance that rules capable of generating languages with the above constraints can and must be ruled out of a theory of natural language.

As of now, we have a number of firm ideas as to the kinds of rules that actually do occur in grammars of natural languages. Constituent structure rules are quite well motivated, as are a number of types of transformational rules: rules that add and delete constants (affixes, prepositions, individual phonological segments, and so on); rules that delete whole constituents under conditions of identity (though it is not altogether clear just what "identity" means); rules that change feature values in certain environments; rules that permute constituents; and so on. However, it is by no means clear at present just how such rules are to be defined, and just what restrictions can or must be placed on them. For instance, it is not at all clear what the metarules for derived constituent structure should be for many kinds of rules. In most transformational grammars that have been published so far, transformational rules have had to be stated with a great many restrictive conditions. For example, some of the rules in Lees [1960] are obligatory if the proper analysis meets one condition, optional if it meets some other condition, and nonapplicable if certain words in a given list appear. So far, no adequate proposal has been made as to how conditions of this sort are to be restricted. In Chapter 3, we shall present an argument to the effect that all such conditions involving individual lexical items or classes of lexical items can be removed from the transformations and either built into individual lexical items in a highly restricted way or built into redundancy rules that operate on lexical items. We shall also see in Chapter 3 that the problem of defining an adequate mechanical procedure for applying rules is a nontrivial one (exclusive of the problem of derived constituent structure), and we shall point out some previously unnoticed areas of difficulty and make some proposals as to how to handle them.

1.5 SOME ASSUMPTIONS

We will assume as background the conception of grammar presented in Noam Chomsky's *Aspects of the Theory of Syntax* [Chomsky, 1965b]. However, there are some particulars in which we disagree with the account of linguistic theory presented there, and there are some ideas that we want to assume that have come to light only since that book was published.

We will present Paul Postal's lexical substitution rule in detail in this section, since it is central to all that follows. As to our other assumptions, we will state them in as short and concise a manner as possible. The reader can find an extensive discussion of them in Appendixes A through E.

1.51 Postal's Lexical Substitution Rule

Chomsky [1965b] takes two positions on lexical substitution. In one, lexical substitution is accomplished by a transformational rule that checks the tree of the simplex into which the lexical item is to be inserted to see that it does not contradict any of the contextual features associated with the item. In the other, complex symbols developed in the base are subcategorized with respect to their immediate environments. Then lexical items are randomly chosen— provided that their contextual features do not contradict the contextual features introduced by subcategorization rules. We will adopt a version of the latter rule that has been suggested by Postal (in lecture, summer 1964).

We assume that the base component of any transformational grammar consists of a set of context-free branching rules and a set of subcategorization rules [see Chomsky, 1965b, Chapter 2]. More precisely, we assume that each occurrence of a lexical category (noun, verb, and so forth) will dominate an ordered pair of feature matrices. The left-hand member of the pair will contain all of the syntactic features introduced by the subcategorization rules of the base. We will refer to such a left-hand member as the "grammatical member" of the pair, and we will call the features contained in it "grammatical features." The right-hand member of the pair will be empty after the operation of the base rules and will be filled later by a lexical item. (1-1) contains an illustration of such an ordered pair, dominated by a lexical category "noun."

$$
\text{NOUN} \tag{1-1}
$$

$$
\begin{bmatrix}
+\text{N (G)} \\
+\text{COUNT (G)} \\
-\text{PRO (G)} \\
+\text{CONCRETE (G)} \\
+\text{SINGULAR (G)} \\
+\text{PHYS. OBJ. (G)} \\
+\text{ANIMATE (G)} \\
+\text{HUMAN (G)}
\end{bmatrix}
$$

[See Remark 1-1.]

After the base rules have generated a P-marker whose terminal elements are ordered pairs as in (1-1), the right-hand member of each ordered pair will be filled by a lexical item chosen at random from the lexicon. We will call this the "lexical member" of the pair, and we will call the features in it "lexical features." When there could be some confusion as to which type of feature we are referring to, we will write a (G) or (L) after the feature in question.

> Grammatical animate feature: [+ANIMATE (G)]
> Lexical animate feature: [+ANIMATE (L)]

We also assume that lexical items will be represented without any redundancies. Thus, *rock* and *boy* might be represented:

(1-2)

> [*rock*, +N (L), +COUNT (L), +PHYS. OBJ. (L),
>   −ANIMATE (L)]
> [*boy*, +N (L), +COUNT (L), +HUMAN, (L)]

where *rock* and *boy* are minimally specified distinctive feature matrices, and the following set of subcategorization rules are assumed:

(1-3)

$$
\text{NOUN} \rightarrow
\begin{bmatrix}
+\text{N} \ (\text{G}) \\[4pt]
\left\{ \begin{matrix} +\text{COUNT} \ (\text{G}) \\ -\text{COUNT} \ (\text{G}) \end{matrix} \right\} \\[4pt]
\left\{ \begin{matrix} +\text{PRO} \ (\text{G}) \\ -\text{PRO} \ (\text{G}) \end{matrix} \right\} \\[4pt]
\left\{ \begin{matrix} +\text{CONCRETE} \ (\text{G}) \\ -\text{CONCRETE} \ (\text{G}) \end{matrix} \right\} \\[4pt]
\left\{ \begin{matrix} +\text{SINGULAR} \ (\text{G}) \\ -\text{SINGULAR} \ (\text{G}) \end{matrix} \right\}
\end{bmatrix}
$$

$$
[+\text{CONCRETE} \ (\text{G})] \rightarrow \left\{ \begin{matrix} [+\text{PHYS. OBJ.} \ (\text{G})] \\ [-\text{PHYS. OBJ.} \ (\text{G})] \end{matrix} \right\}
$$

$$
[+\text{PHYS. OBJ.} \ (\text{G})] \rightarrow \left\{ \begin{matrix} [+\text{ANIMATE} \ (\text{G})] \\ [-\text{ANIMATE} \ (\text{G})] \end{matrix} \right\}
$$

$$
[+\text{ANIMATE} \ (\text{G})] \rightarrow \left\{ \begin{matrix} [+\text{HUMAN} \ (\text{G})] \\ [-\text{HUMAN} \ (\text{G})] \end{matrix} \right\}
$$

where [ ] indicates a feature matrix and {   } indicates an optional choice.

Suppose that the lexical items of (1-2) are substituted into the right-hand side of the pair in (1-1). The result would be:

a. NOUN (1-4)

$$
\begin{bmatrix}
\text{+N (G)} & \text{+N (L)} \\
\text{+COUNT (G)} & \text{+COUNT (L)} \\
\text{−PRO (G)} & \\
\text{+CONCRETE (G)} & \\
\text{+SINGULAR (G)} & \\
\text{+PHYS. OBJ. (G)} & \text{+PHYS. OBJ. (L)} \\
\text{+ANIMATE (G)} & \text{−ANIMATE (L)} \\
\text{+HUMAN (G)} & \\
& \textit{, rock}
\end{bmatrix}
$$

b. NOUN

$$
\begin{bmatrix}
\text{+N (G)} & \text{+N (L)} \\
\text{+COUNT (G)} & \text{+COUNT (L)} \\
\text{−PRO (G)} & \\
\text{+CONCRETE (G)} & \\
\text{+SINGULAR (G)} & \\
\text{+PHYS. OBJ. (G)} & \\
\text{+ANIMATE (G)} & \\
\text{+HUMAN (G)} & \text{+HUMAN (L)} \\
& \textit{, boy}
\end{bmatrix}
$$

In b all of the lexical features of *boy* agree in sign with the grammatical features of the complex symbol developed by the base. When this is the case, we will say that the grammatical and lexical members of the pair are *compatible* (or in Chomsky's terminology, *nondistinct*). In a, the lexical feature [−ANIMATE (L)] of *rock* is incompatible with the grammatical feature [−ANIMATE (G)] of the complex symbol developed by the base. When the lexical member of a pair is incompatible with the grammatical member of a pair, we will say that the pair defines a "violation." Any sentence generated by the grammar with one or more violations we will define as being "ungrammatical." Note that we could extend this definition in a natural way to define degrees of grammaticality in terms of the number and types of violations. [See Appendix B.] Since the selectional features on VERBS are defined in terms of the grammatical features, not the lexical features, of nouns, the choice of *boy* in (1-4b) will lead to grammatical sentences in an adequate grammar of English. For example,

The boy saw me coming.
His tricks amazed the boy.

However, the choice of *rock* in (1-4a) will lead to ungrammatical sentences in the same contexts:

* The rock saw me coming.
* His tricks amazed the rock.

In the case of grammatical sentences, the lexical substitution rule that we have just defined is entirely equivalent to that defined by Chomsky [1965b, 2.3.3]. What this lexical substitution rule does is to extend the notion of a filter given by Chomsky [1965a and b] so that each grammar will not only generate the fully grammatical sentences of the language it defines, but also directly generate a great many of the partially grammatical or ungrammatical sentences and mark them as such.

1.52 Violation and Contradiction

Note that a violation, as we have defined it, is analogous to the notion of contradiction in symbolic logic. Consider each complex symbol not just as a set of features, but as a conjunction of features. For each feature, F, interpret [−F] as the negation of [+F], that is, [−F] = not [+F]. Interpret the operation of comparing the signs of the lexical and grammatical features as the conjunction of the two complex symbols. Thus, in the case of (1-4a) the grammatical feature [+ANIMATE] will be conjoined with the lexical feature [−ANIMATE]. Since [−ANIMATE] = not [+ANIMATE], we get

[+ANIMATE] and not [+ANIMATE]

which is of the form

P and not P

and hence defines a contradiction. This interpretation will turn out to be very useful below, when we extend our definition of a lexical item.

1.53 Other Assumptions

In much of what follows we will assume that what have traditionally been called adjectives and verbs are members of a single lexical category (which we will call VERB) and differ only by a single syntactic feature (which we will call ADJECTIVAL). However, the bulk of our argument does not depend strongly on this assumption, and so we shall not attempt to demonstrate it conclusively. But since some may feel that this assertion is a radical one, we are including an appendix in which we present a case for its plausibility. [See Appendix A.]

Thus we will represent adjectives as:

$$
\begin{bmatrix}
\text{VERB} \\
+\text{V} \\
+\text{ADJECTIVAL}
\end{bmatrix}
$$

Verbs will be represented as:

$$
\begin{bmatrix}
\text{VERB} \\
+\text{V} \\
-\text{ADJECTIVAL}
\end{bmatrix}
$$

We will also assume a notion of "normality" or "markedness" for syntactic features. This notion states that each feature has a "normal" and a "nonnormal" value, given the values of other features. For instance, it is "normal" for [−COUNT] nouns to be [+SINGULAR] (for example, *milk, clay,* and so on). It is "nonnormal" for [−COUNT] nouns to be [−SINGULAR] (for example, *pants*).

We will attempt to capture the notion of normality by assuming that syntactic features are represented in the lexicon not in terms of pluses and minuses, but only in terms of whether or not they are normal. Thus, the SINGULAR feature for *clay* will be represented as normal, but the SINGULAR feature for *pants* will be represented as nonnormal. We will then have rules to convert the binary features, normal and nonnormal, into pluses and minuses. In order to capture the notion that a lexicon is more regular if it has fewer nonnormal features, our evaluation measure will count only nonnormal feature values. That is, only nonnormal values will contribute to the complexity of the lexicon. When we get to the discussion of exceptions to syntactic rules, the notion of normality will have a clear interpretation—exceptions will be nonnormal, regular cases will be normal.

In the discussion that follows, we will represent normal feature values with a *u* (for "unmarked") and nonnormal values with an *m* (for "marked"). Thus, the normal value for the feature SINGULAR will be represented: [u SINGULAR]. The nonnormal value will be represented: [m SINGULAR].

[For a further discussion of "normality" (or "markedness") and the empirical basis of this notion, see Appendix C.]

We will also assume that contextual features are analyzable, rather than being unanalyzable as suggested by Chomsky [1965b, pp. 118–120]. That is, a verb that takes animate subjects and abstract objects will be represented with the two analyzable features: [+[+ANIMATE]__] and [+__[+ABSTRACT]], rather than the unanalyzable: [+[+ANIMATE]__[+ABSTRACT]]. Moreover, we will assume that lexical items may contain Boolean functions of features. For a discussion of these matters, see Appendixes D and E.

2 PREVIOUS WORK

2.1 ARBITRARY SUBCATEGORIZATION

In all of the published work on transformational grammar, only one device has been utilized for handling irregularities: arbitrary subcategorization. If most words in a class had to undergo a rule, while a few exceptions could not undergo it, it was assumed that further subcategorization was necessary and that the exceptions formed a subclass of their own, to be distinguished from the regularities by a separate syntactic feature. For simplicity, let us take an example from phonology. There is a rule in English that makes tense vowels lax in the syllable before the suffix *-ity* (providing that there is an intervening consonant). Since this rule occurred in the grammar before the contemporary rules that reflect the great vowel shift, it, together with the vowel shift rules, is responsible for the vowel alternations in *obscene-obscenity, vain-vanity, divine-divinity, profound-profundity,* and many others. One of the very few exceptions to this rule is *obese.* It yields [obīysity], not [obĕsity]. No other fact about *obese* is correlated to the fact that it does not undergo this rule. It is simply an isolated fact.

With only the device of arbitrary subcategorization in our linguistic theory, we would have to handle *obese* in the following way. We would have to conjure up an arbitrary feature, perhaps called "shortening." Normal words like *obscene, vain, divine,* and so on would have to be marked in the lexicon as "plus shortening." *Obese* would be marked as "minus shortening." The rule would then have to be made somewhat less general, so that it would apply only to "plus shortening" vowels.

The shortcomings of such a solution are fairly obvious. The feature "shortening" serves no other purpose than to distinguish an isolated exception to a rule from those normal words that undergo the rule. It would never be mentioned anywhere else in a grammar of English. This is disturbing on a number of counts. First, we would have to revise our tentative universal theory of language to include the feature "shortening" as one of those features that can possibly occur in a grammar of a natural language. But it seems absurd to set up a given feature as a universal if it occurs only once in only one language and then serves only to distinguish a handful of exceptions to a single rule of the language. But even if such a feature played an important role in a wide variety of languages, it would be questionable to set up as a functioning property of English a feature that would play no role at all if a handful of words were lost from the language.

But there are even more serious difficulties here. The device of arbitrary subcategorization fails to capture two notions that an adequate theory of language should capture.

1. A theory of language should provide a way for grammars defined by that theory to distinguish exceptions from regular cases. Thus, an irregularity like *obese* should be formally distinguished in a grammar of English from regular cases like *vain, divine,* and so on.

2. A theory of language should provide an evaluation measure that prefers grammars with few exceptions to those with many exceptions. That is, the grammar that points out the most regularities should be preferred. In terms of the only evaluation measures that have been proposed so far—those that map generality inversely into length—we would expect exceptions to count more than nonexceptional cases. Thus, all other things being equal, the grammar with the greater number of exceptions would have the greater length.

Clearly, these conditions are not independent. Condition 2 depends on Condition 1, since you must be able to tell what items are exceptions before you can assign numbers to them. Thus, to show that arbitrary subcategorization fails both conditions, it is sufficient to show that it fails Condition 1.

Consider the case of *obese*. The only way that our theory allowed us to distinguish *obese* as an exception to Rule *n* was to mark it with respect to a special feature, which we called "shortening." We decided to assign *obese* minus and the regular cases, the value plus, with respect to this feature. The only way that we could pick out the exceptions with respect to this rule by looking at the lexicon would be by the fact that they were marked minus with respect to this special feature, while the regular cases were marked plus. Since this distinction seems to form the only basis on which this theory might be made to meet Condition 1, we could set up a tentative proposal based on it. One logical proposal would be the following:

> *Proposal 1:* Amend Theory I in the following way: establish in it a special vocabulary of arbitrary features, which will be used to mark exceptions. Then, in a grammar defined by Theory I', a lexical item marked minus with respect to one of these arbitrary features will constitute an exception.

There is one immediate difficulty with Proposal 1. Again consider the case of *obese*. Since the exception features are arbitrarily chosen, they may be given arbitrary values. Thus, we could have called our exception feature for Rule *n* "nonshortening" instead of "shortening" and correspondingly marked *obese* plus nonshortening instead of minus shortening. Since the choice of each value for each possible arbitrary feature is arbitrary, we could perfectly well have a situation where the irregularities with respect to one arbitrary feature were marked plus, while those with respect to another feature were marked minus. This would not allow us to characterize exceptions in the lexicon according to Proposal 1.

To get Proposal 1 to work, we would have to be able to guarantee that all exceptions were marked in the same way—all minus or all plus. That is, we need a way of regularizing the marking of exception features. Note that when we decide that exceptions to a rule will be marked minus for some arbitrary feature, the plus value for that feature must be added to the structural description of the rule in question. Thus, we had to revise Rule *n* so that it referred to tense vowels that were marked plus shortening. We can use this fact to amend our theory in such a way as to regularize the marking of exceptions.

> *Proposal 2:* Amend theory I as follows: only the plus value of an exception feature may appear in the structural description of a rule.

Proposal 2, together with Proposal 1, will enable us to regularize the marking of exceptions for cases like Rule *n:* an item marked minus for an exception feature would be an exception. If all rules were like Rule *n,* and if all exceptions were like *obese,* then Proposals 1 and 2 would allow us to characterize exceptions using arbitrary subcategorization. Moreover, there would be a natural sort of evaluation measure for exception features, namely, count the exception features marked minus, but not those marked plus. Since the exception features marked plus indicate regularities, while those marked minus indicate exceptions, this measure simply says count the exceptions, not the regularities. Such an evaluation measure will prefer grammars with the fewest exceptions.

Unfortunately, not all exceptions are like *obese,* cases where a very general rule does not apply in isolated cases. Consider cases like *foot-feet, mouse-mice, louse-lice, tooth-teeth, goose-geese.* In these cases, the plural is formed by a rule that makes tense, grave vowels in Germanic words nongrave (Rule *k*). But Rule *k* is not a productive rule; items that undergo Rule *k* are not ordinary cases, but exceptions. Ordinary cases like *boot, soup, suit, lout, bout, juice,* and so on do not undergo Rule *k*.

The existence of rules like *k* makes it impossible to maintain Proposals 1 and 2 and still characterize exceptions in terms of arbitrary subcategorization. Proposals 1 and 2 require that the value of the arbitrary feature indicating the exception be opposite that of the feature mentioned in the rule. For rules like *k*, however, the reverse is true. Let us call our arbitrary feature "umlaut." If Rule *k* is revised so that it applies to grave, tense vowels in Germanic words marked plus umlaut, then items like *tooth* and *mouse* must be marked plus umlaut if the rule is to apply to them. For nonproductive rules like *k*, the exceptions and the structural description must be marked in the *same* way with respect to the arbitrary feature involved. It is the regular cases such as *house* whose arbitrary features must not coincide in value with the corresponding feature mentioned in the structural description. For this reason, Proposals 1 and 2 cannot be maintained. It seems, then, that if our tentative theory of language is to meet Conditions 1 and 2, it must be revised to include some more powerful devices for handling exceptions.

2.2 THE CHOMSKY-HALLE SYSTEM

Noam Chomsky and Morris Halle, in *The Sound Pattern of English,* have devised the following way of dealing with irregularities in phonology. They assume that each morpheme will be subcategorized with respect to each phonological rule. That is, they assume that linguistic theory defines a set of "rule features" for each grammar, each rule feature referring to one rule of the given grammar. Suppose a lexical morpheme is an exception to a rule, say Rule 73. The morpheme will be entered in the lexicon marked [−R73]. Everything that is not an exception would be marked [+R73]. The evaluation procedure would count the minus-valued rule features, not the plus-valued ones. Thus, it would value more highly grammars with fewer exceptions.

By claiming that rule features are associated with entire morphemes, Chomsky and Halle are making a rather strong assertion: it will never be the case that one segment in a morpheme will be an exception to a rule while another segment is not; either all segments are exceptions to a given rule, or no segments are. So far, no counterexamples to this assertion have been uncovered.

In incorporating rule features into linguistic theory, Chomsky and Halle have adopted the following conventions:

No rule feature may be mentioned in the structural (2-1) description of a rule.

All morphemic features, including rule features, are (2-2) projected by a mechanical procedure into each phonological segment.

If Rule n is a phonological rule, then it may not apply (2-3) to a segment marked [—Rule n].

A theory of language incorporating these conventions can handle cases like *obesity* [see Section 2.1]. *Obesity* would be marked minus for the rule that makes vowels lax before *-ity*. The rule, without modification, will then fail to apply to *obese,* though it will apply in all normal cases. In general, such a theory can handle cases where exceptional individual items cannot undergo obligatory rules.

The theory, as stated so far, cannot handle two common cases in phonology: (1) Cases where an otherwise very general rule does not apply in some simply stated environment; to take a hypothetical example, consider a case in which a penultimate vowel is shortened unless preceded by an /h/. (2) Cases like *foot-feet* [see Section 1.1] in which a rule does not generally apply, but applies only in isolated cases.

In order to handle cases like (1), Chomsky and Halle set up the following device. They allow rules that say that the next rule does not apply in some environment. That is, they allow rules equivalent to those of the following form:

Rule $k:$ [   ] → [—Rule $k{+}1$]/ in some environment   (2-4)

Thus, in case (1) above, suppose that the vowel shortening rule were Rule 89. Rule 88 would read:

Rule 88: [   ] → [—Rule 89]/h___   (2-5)

Although Chomsky and Halle did not set up their system to account for cases like (2), we can handle such cases in their system by using a null environment in a rule of the form of (2-4). Suppose the rule that produces *geese* from *goose* is Rule 374. Rule 373 would then read:

Rule 373: [   ] → [—Rule 374]   (2-6)

This says that all normal words do not undergo Rule 374. Cases like *goose* can now be looked at as exceptions to Rule 373, rather than to Rule 374. That is, we can mark *goose* [—Rule 373] in the lexicon. It, like all normal words, will be marked [+Rule 374]. Unlike normal words, *goose* will not undergo Rule 373, will remain marked [+Rule 374], and will undergo Rule 374.

Note the differences between this system and use of arbitrary subcategorization:

1. Arbitrary features can now be eliminated from the universal vocabulary of the theory of language. Instead, the theory, given a grammar, automatically defines an appropriate set of rule features.

2. This system provides what seems to be an adequate definition of the notion of exception to a phonological rule. It also provides an evaluation measure that values grammars with few exceptions more highly than grammars with many exceptions.

3. This system makes the claim that exceptions to phonological rules are morphemic in nature, rather than segmental. It also makes the claim that all exceptions to phonological rules can be represented within the system in terms of negatively specified rule features. We will see in Chapters 6, 7, and 8 that this system cannot be simply extended to syntax and still provide an adequate definition of an exception. However, we shall find that the notion of rule features of this sort will be indispensable in handling syntactic exceptions.

3

SIMPLE EXCEPTIONS

3.1 ITEMS THAT DO NOT UNDERGO REGULAR RULES

When a lexical item may not undergo an obligatory rule even though it may meet the structural description of the rule, we will call that word a "simple exception." As we saw in the last chapter, *obesity* is such a case in phonology. Parallel examples in syntax are quite common. Consider the verbs that do not undergo the passive transformation; for example, *resemble, owe, have, possess, equal.*

a. John resembles Mary's mother.
   * Mary's mother is resembled by John.
b. John owes two dollars.
   * Two dollars are owed by John.
c. Mary had a horse.
   * A horse was had by Mary.
d. John possessed a cow.
   * A cow was possessed by John.
e. Two and two equal four.
   * Four is equalled by two and two.
f. I meant what I said.
   * What I said was meant by me.
g. I wanted a catcher's mitt.
   * A catcher's mitt was wanted by me.

There is no independently motivated syntactic class that distinguishes these verbs from those that do undergo the passive. It is simply an idiosyncratic fact about these verbs that they do not undergo that rule. This is not obvious [see Appendix F for discussion].

A great number of verbs can undergo the rule that forms agentive nominals. For example,

    a. John was one who transgressed against the law of the land.
       John was a transgressor against the law of the land.
    b. John was the one who killed the deer.
       John was the killer of the deer.
    c. John is one who imports rugs.
       John is an importer of rugs.

However, some verbs cannot form agentive nominals.

    a. John Gurk is one who used to massacre Indians.
       * John Gurk used to be a massacrer of Indians.
    b. John was the one who knew that fact.
       *John was the knower of that fact.
    c. John was the one who struck Bill.
       * John was the striker of Bill.

Again, there is no independently motivated syntactic property that distinguishes those that do undergo the rule from those that do not.

Most verbs have their following prepositions deleted when they are not nominalized. [For example, see Section A.1 and example (A-3) in Appendix A.] A number of verbs, such as *decide on, depend on, consist of,* and so on, do not undergo this rule and keep their prepositions. Again, this fact cannot be predicted from any independently motivated properties of these verbs.

Cases of the same sort turns up in morphology as well as in syntax. For example, the usual agentive suffix in English is *er: hit-hitter, kill-killer, murder-murderer, bowl-bowler, golf-golfer,* and so on. However, there are some agent nouns corresponding to existing verbs that do not take any suffix: *pilot, cook, boss, nag,* and so on. Similarly, most plural words take a plural ending in English. *Sheep* does not. If we assume that endings are spelled out on the ends of words by very late rules of the grammar, then these cases are items that simply cannot undergo this rule.

In transformational grammars as they have appeared in all the work published so far, such exceptions to rules are either handled by arbitrary subcategorization or must appear in lists of exceptions that are tacked on as conditions to the rule in question. We would like to avoid both of these devices: arbitrary subcategorization for the reasons mentioned in Section 2.1 and the listing of exceptions for two reasons. (1) It does not seem to be part of a *rule* of a language that certain isolated words are exceptions to that rule; rather, it seems to be idiosyncratic information about individual lexical items. Since the lexicon, by definition, is set up to contain all idiosyncratic facts about individual items, we should like to build this information into the lexical representation of those items. (2) We would like to put as many constraints as possible on the form of a possible transformational rule. One natural sort of constraint is that a rule should refer only to grammatical categories and properties and not to individual lexical items. We would like to see if such a constraint is possible and, if so, what it involves.

3.2 THE DIRECT GENERATION OF DEVIANT SENTENCES

Exceptions of the above sort—where general rules do not apply to isolated lexical items—can be handled by a formalism like that set up by Chomsky and Halle to handle phonological exceptions. We can allow lexical items to be subcategorized with respect to all the rules of the grammar. When an item cannot undergo a rule, we will mark it minus for that rule feature. Otherwise, all rule features will be marked plus. In order to have our theory favor grammars with the fewest exceptions, we will count only the minus-valued rule features, not the plus-valued ones. In order to keep rules from applying to exceptions, we will define a rule so that it applies only to plus-valued items. These are exactly the conventions that Chomsky and Halle use in phonology; and if we are concerned only with characterizing the completely grammatical sentences of a language, these conventions will work for the kind of exceptions we encountered in Section 3.1.

However, if we follow Postal's suggestion (in lecture, summer 1964) that grammars be constructed so that they generate directly not only the fully grammatical sentences of the language, but also the partially grammatical ones, marking them automatically as to the degree and nature of their deviance, then the Chomsky-Halle conventions will have to be extended. We will expand upon these conventions by utilizing the apparatus suggested by Postal in his revision of Chomsky's lexical substitution rule. [See Section 1.51.] In essence, we will consider the rule features specified in a lexical item as stating a set of conditions that must be met by the grammatical member of any complex symbol into which it is inserted.

At this point our choice of the Postal system is dictated more by esthetic considerations than by necessity. Since a linguistic theory must characterize partially grammatical sentences as well as fully grammatical ones, it seems esthetically pleasing to devise a system in which each grammar will do so directly. However, as we shall see in Chapter 8 below, this choice is motivated by factual as well as esthetic considerations. It is a necessary choice, not an arbitrary one.

Note that Chomsky and Halle, in counting minus-valued rule features, but not plus-valued ones, are utilizing a partial equivalent of the concept of markedness (minus is marked, plus is unmarked). As we shall see in Chapter 5, the use of minuses and pluses rather than *m*'s and *u*'s for this purpose fails for the description of exceptions in the same way as it fails in phonology and syntax. Rather than adopt the plus-minus notations now and switch to *m* and *u* later, we will use the *m-u* notation from the start.

3.3 A PARTIAL FORMALISM FOR SIMPLE EXCEPTIONS

We will extend our definition of the grammatical member of the complex symbol in the following way:

1. The grammatical member of each complex symbol will be subcategorized with respect to each transformational rule of the grammar. In the deep structure, the grammatical member will be marked minus for each rule feature. Thus, [−R(23)] means that Rule 23 has not applied. When a rule applies (that is, when the structural change of a rule is carried out), the value of the corresponding rule feature will automatically be changed from minus to plus by a metarule of the theory of grammar. If Rule 23 applies, the grammatical member of the appropriate complex symbol will contain the feature [+R(23)]. (The notion of appropriateness will be taken up in Chapter 4.)

2. The grammatical member of each complex symbol will also be subcategorized with respect to the *structural description* of each transformational rule of the grammar. Thus, grammatical members will contain both rule features and structural description features. As it leaves the base, each grammatical member will be marked minus for each structural description feature. Thus, [−SD(23)] will mean that the structural description of Rule 23 has not yet been met. When the structural description of a rule is met, a metarule of the theory of grammar will change the structural description feature from minus to plus. If the structural description of Rule 23 is met, the grammatical member will contain the feature [+SD(23)]. Since, by the definition of a rule, the structural

change of a rule can take place only if the structural description is met, it will make no sense for an SD feature to be marked minus, while its corresponding R feature is marked plus. That is, the combination of features [—SD(75)] and [+R(75)] will never occur.

So far, we have given no justification for the introduction of structural description features. Though they are not necessary for the description of the phenomena we have considered so far, we shall see in Chapter 6 that they are necessary for the description of certain types of irregularities. We introduce them now only so that we will not have to change our notation later.

As things now stand, each complex symbol, as it comes out of the base, is marked minus in its grammatical member for all structural description and rule features. A lexical item is then chosen, and the transformational rules are applied. With respect to the SD and R features, derivations will proceed as follows: Consider an arbitrary rule, say Rule 47. Before Rule 47 is reached in the course of a derivation, each grammatical member will contain:

[—SD(47)] and [—R(47)]

If the structural description of Rule 47 is met, the following meta-rule will apply:

For all rules i, if the structural description of i is met:
[—SD(i)] → [+SD(i)]

The result will be:

[+SD(47)] and [—R(47)]

At this point the rule may freely apply or not apply. If the structural change of Rule 47 is carried out, the grammatical member of the appropriate complex symbol will contain:

[+SD(47)] and [+R(47)]

In standardizing the operation of a rule, we will assume that obligatory rules are basic. As stated above, if the structural description of a rule is met, then the rule may freely operate or not operate. Given the above conventions, we will have to set up definitions so that the following will hold:

1. Suppose the structural change is carried out.   (3-1)
    a. If the relevant lexical item was not an exception to the rule, then no violation should result. (The rule should have applied, and did.)
    b. If the relevant lexical item was an exception to the rule, there should be a violation. (The rule applied when it should not have.)

2. Suppose the structural change is not carried out.
    a. If the lexical item was not an exception to the rule, then a violation should result. (The obligatory rule did not apply when it should have.)
    b. If the lexical item was an exception to the rule, then no violation should result. (The rule should not have applied, and it did not.)

We will represent exceptions in lexical items using the notion of "normality" and conventions concerning markedness. "Normality" has a completely natural interpretation in terms of exceptions to rules. It is not "normal" for an item to be an exception to a rule; it is "normal" for an item not to be an exception to a rule. An exception to Rule i will be marked ($[m\ R(i)]$) in the lexicon; a normal case (a nonexception to Rule i) will be unmarked ($[u\ R(i)]$). Our evaluation measure will count marked features, and not count unmarked ones.

For the moment we will not consider what it might mean for an item to have a marked structural description feature, and we will temporarily assume that all lexical items are unmarked for all structural description features. Thus, a lexical item that is normal with respect to, say, Rule 89 will have the features:

$[u\ SD(89)]$ and $[u\ R(89)]$.

An exception to Rule 89 will have the features:

$[u\ SD(89)]$ and $[m\ R(89)]$.

So far, the conventions we have described yield the possibilities of (3-2) below. (G) indicates that the feature is in the grammatical member; (L), that it is in the lexical member. In the a sentences the structural description for Rule 89 has not been met, and Rule 89, of course, has not operated. In b, the SD has been met, but the rule has not operated. In c, the SD has been met and the rule has operated. Sentence 1 contains an ordinary lexical item ($[u\ R(89)$ (L)]$); 2 contains an exception to Rule 89 as its lexical member ($[m\ R(89)$ (L)]$).

(3-2)

1. a. [−SD(89) (G)]   [u SD(89) (L)]
     [−R(89) (G)]   [u R(89) (L)]   no violation

   b. [+SD(89) (G)]   [u SD(89) (L)]
     [−R(89) (G)]   [u R(89) (L)]   VIOLATION

   c. [+SD(89) (G)]   [u SD(89) (L)]
     [+R(89) (G)]   [u R(89) (L)]   no violation

2. a. [−SD(89) (G)]   [u SD(89) (L)]
     [−R(89) (G)]   [m R(89) (L)]   no violation

   b. [+SD(89) (G)]   [u SD(89) (L)]
     [−R(89) (G)]   [m R(89) (L)]   no violation

   c. [+SD(89) (G)]   [u SD(89) (L)]
     [+R(89) (G)]   [m R(89) (L)]   VIOLATION

In 1.b, the rule has not applied when it should have. In 2.c, the rule has applied when it should not have.

We now need a set of metarules to convert the u's and m's into pluses and minuses so that violations will occur where they should occur and will not occur where they should not. The following is one possible set of such metarules. It occurs at the *end* of the grammar, can be looked upon as a device that checks the lexical markings (m's and u's) in the sentence against the relevant derivational history of the sentence, determines whether any conditions were broken, and then sorts out the fully grammatical sentences from the partially grammatical ones.

Metarule 1. For all rules i.   (3-3)
[m R(i) (L)] → [−R(i) (L)]

In all lexical items, marked rule features assume the value minus.

Metarule 3. For all rules i.   (3-4)
[u SD(i) (L)] → [α SD(i) (L)] / [__, α SD(i) (G)]

Each unmarked structural description feature in the lexical member assumes the value of the corresponding structural description feature in the grammatical member. Since we are not considering marked SD features here, this rule may seem vacuous. We shall see later that it is not. It says, essentially, that unmarked SD features can never contribute to a violation.

Metarule 5. For all rules i.   (3-5)
[u R(i) (L)] → [α R(i) (L)] / [__, α SD(i) (L)]

Each unmarked rule feature of the lexical member assumes the value of the corresponding SD feature of the lexical member. Metarule 5 simply states that for all nonexceptional lexical items, an obligatory rule must apply if its structural description is met and, of course, not apply if its structural description is not met.

These metarules map the lexical features of (3-2) into those of (3-6).

(3-6)

1. a. $[-SD(89) \quad (G)]$ $[-SD(89) \quad (L)]$
    $[-R(89) \quad (G)]$ $[-R(89) \quad (L)]$ no violation

   b. $[+SD(89) \quad (G)]$ $[+SD(89) \quad (L)]$
    $[-R(89) \quad (G)]$ $[+R(89) \quad (L)]$ VIOLATION

   c. $[+SD(89) \quad (G)]$ $[+SD(89) \quad (L)]$
    $[+R(89) \quad (G)]$ $[+R(89) \quad (L)]$ no violation

2. a. $[-SD(89) \quad (G)]$ $[-SD(89) \quad (L)]$
    $[-R(89) \quad (G)]$ $[-R(89) \quad (L)]$ no violation

   b. $[+SD(89) \quad (G)]$ $[+SD(89) \quad (L)]$
    $[-R(89) \quad (G)]$ $[-R(89) \quad (L)]$ no violation

   c. $[+SD(89) \quad (G)]$ $[+SD(89) \quad (L)]$
    $[+R(89) \quad (G)]$ $[-R(89) \quad (L)]$ VIOLATION

Violations occur in cases 1.b and 2.c, where the value of the lexical rule feature is incompatible with that of the grammatical rule feature. Thus, we can extend to cases like this the definition of a violation given in Section 3.3 above. That is, we have a violation when a lexical rule feature is incompatible with its corresponding grammatical feature.

4 RULE GOVERNMENT

We have assumed so far that as each transformation operates; the fact that it has done so is recorded in one or more "appropriate" complex symbols in the sentence being derived. In the case of phonological rules it was clear which complex symbols were the appropriate ones, namely those in which the phonological changes took place. In syntax, the case is not so clear, since syntactic transformations may be global as well as local, that is, they may perform structural changes on indefinitely large branches of trees. Are we to assume that every complex symbol in a branch of a tree that undergoes the structural change of a rule is to be marked as having undergone that rule? Clearly not. Consider the sentence

> The boy who resembled his mother was beaten up by (4-1)
> the gang.

(4-1) has undergone the passive transformation (more precisely, its matrix S has undergone it). Both the subject and object noun phrases have undergone a structural change. In particular, *the boy who resembled his mother* has been shifted to the front of the sentence. If we mark each complex symbol in this noun phrase as having undergone the passive transformation, then among other things, we will have to mark *resemble* as having undergone the passive. But *resemble* is an exception to the passive; if it undergoes the passive, we should get a violation Yet we do not get one; (4-1) is fully grammatical. So our tentative hypothesis is incorrect.

If it is false that every complex symbol in a branch which undergoes the structural change of a rule must be marked for having undergone the rule, then is it true that some such complex symbol must be so marked? Or is it true that only a complex symbol in a branch that has been changed *may* be so marked? The answer to both questions seems to be no.

It is easy to see that this is so. Recall that we mentioned that such verbs as *resemble* are exceptions in that they cannot undergo the passive transformation, unlike most transitive verbs, which can undergo the passive. Note that it makes perfectly good sense to speak of a verb undergoing the passive. Note also that the passive transformation *does not change the verb at all:* it interchanges the subject and object and adds BE+EN to the auxiliary. Since this is so, why does it make sense to speak of the verb as "undergoing" the passive transformation?

In some sense, the verb "governs" the passive transformation; it is central to the operation of the rule. [See Remark 4-1.] There are a number of other clear cases where it is obvious which item it is that governs a rule. Most of these involve verbs. The rules that define most major sentence phenomena, for example, questions, imperatives, negatives, reflexives, and so on, are governed by verbs (or more properly, VERBS). We speak of VERBS that may or may not be questioned, may or may not take the imperative, reflexive, passive, and so on. This way of speaking seems to reflect our intuitions as to which items are central to certain rules.

This intuitive notion of "government" seems to correspond to the notion of a possible exception. Just as verbs are the only possible exceptions to the passive transformation, so only a verb could be an exception to the question transformation. (For example, *beware:* *Did you beware of John?) One could not imagine a noun or a preposition being an exception to the question transformation.

The notion of possible exception and the notion of what must be marked when a rule operates seem to come together in the partly intuitive notion of government. Government, of course, is not yet a completely well-defined notion, and we can offer no proposal for an adequate definition of it. There are, however, a large number of clear cases of government, which we will assume in the remainder of this work. The closest thing to a generalization that we can offer is that the main VERB (the most dominant VERB in the S under consideration) governs a great many rules. But, as we shall see below, there are exceptions to this principle that we are at a loss to formalize.

Note that in "spelling" rules—rules that give phonological shape (suffixes, prefixes, and so on) to syntactic features of lexical categories—the item that governs the rule is invariably the stem to which the phonological shape is attached. For example, nouns govern the rule that places plural endings on nouns. Thus, certain noun stems may be exceptions: that is, *child, sheep, ox,* and so on.

Government seems to be an important notion in grammar, and our inability to define it precisely points up our ignorance of certain major aspects of grammatical theory. One of the things required of linguistic theory is characterization of government. That is, the theory must be able to define a mechanical procedure such that, given as input a transformational rule and the tree it is operating on, the procedure will find the item in the tree which governs the rule. Note that such a procedure would associate with each rule at least one terminal symbol (CS) associated with a lexical category in each tree which could meet the structural description of the rule. To insist upon such a procedure would be to limit strongly the class of possible grammars.

5 MINOR RULES

5.1 RULES THAT APPLY ONLY TO EXCEPTIONS

As we pointed out in Section 3.1, there are certain rules in English that apply only to exceptions and not to ordinary lexical items. We will call them "minor rules." The example we mentioned was the rule that formed the plurals of *foot, mouse, louse,* and so on. Rules of this sort also occur in syntax.

5.11 Not-Transportation

For example, there is an optional rule in English (which we will call NOT-TRANSPORTATION) that moves a *not* from an embedded object complement to the main verb of the matrix sentence. Consider the following:

1. a. I think that John didn't come.   (5-1)
   b. I don't think that John came.
2. a. I believe that John won't come.
   b. I don't believe that John will come.
3. a. I anticipate that John won't come.
   b. I don't anticipate that John will come.

Each of the b sentences is ambiguous in that the *not* may either be introduced in the deep structure of the matrix sentence or may be transformed from its position in the corresponding a sentence. That is, each b sentence, on one reading, is understood in the same way as its corresponding a sentence.

The NOT-TRANSPORTATION rule operates on only a handful of verbs like *think, believe, anticipate, expect, want,* and so on; it does not operate on most verbs that take object complements, such as *hope, like, hate, require, request, show,* and so forth.

(Note, by the way, that the matrix verb governs NOT-TRANS-PORTATION.)

Another rule that operates only on exceptions, not on regular verbs, is the FLIP rule [see A.6]. Although this rule applies to more than a handful of verbs (*amaze, amuse, surprise, appall, benefit, please, satisfy,* and so on), most transitive verbs do not undergo the rule (for example, *fear, hope, believe, desire, want, regret, like, know, consider, think, expect,* . . .), and there is no independently motivated way of predicting which verbs can undergo the rule. (Note that the matrix VERB governs FLIP.)

5.12 Object Nominalization

Another such rule is the one that forms objective nominals. We will call it OBJ-NOM. OBJ-NOM forms nouns that refer to the objects of verbs. For example,

a. things that John did ⟹ John's deeds   (5-2)
b. things that John told ⟹ John's tales
c. that which John vomited ⟹ John's vomit
d. that which John barfed ⟹ John's barf
e. that which John sweated ⟹ John's sweat
f. that which John perspired ⟹ John's perspiration
g. those whom we imprisoned ⟹ our prisoners
h. those things that we believe ⟹ our beliefs
i. those things that John wrote ⟹ John's writings
j. those things that Picasso painted ⟹ Picasso's paintings
k. those whom IBM employs ⟹ IBM's employees
l. those whom John tutors ⟹ John's tutees

Most transitive verbs, however, do not undergo this rule. Again there is no independently motivated way of predicting which verbs will and which will not undergo the rule.

5.13 Instrumental Nominalization

Instrumental nominals are another case in point. There is a rule in English for creating names of instruments from the verbs denoting the functions they are to perform. (Call the rule INSTR-NOM.) For example,

a. a device with which one slices things ⟹ a slicer   (5-3)
b. a device with which one mixes things ⟹ a mixer
c. a device with which one refrigerates things ⟹ a refrigerator
d. a device with which one freezes things ⟹ a freezer
e. a device with which one projects things ⟹ a projector

    f. a device with which one computes things ⇒ a computer
    g. a device with which one heats things ⇒ a heater

As is quite obvious, most verbs that can take instrumentals do not undergo this rule. Thus, we do not get:

    a. a device with which one kills someone ⇏ a killer   (5-4)
    b. a device with which one sees something ⇏ a seer
    c. a device with which one hits something ⇏ a hitter

and so on.

5.14 ABLE Substitution

The rule which forms *readable* from *able to be read* is also a minor rule. (Call it ABLE-SUB.) Thus we get:

    a. His handwriting can be read ⇒ His handwriting   (5-5) is readable
    b. He can be depended upon ⇒ He is dependable
    c. The present can be returned ⇒ The present is returnable
    d. This function can be computed ⇒ This function is computable
    e. This condition can be satisfied ⇒ This condition is satisfiable
    f. John can be relied upon ⇒ John is reliable

Most verbs, however, cannot undergo this rule. Thus we do not get:

    a. John can be killed ⇏ *John is killable   (5-6)
    b. John can be shot ⇏ *John is shootable
    c. His fast ball can be hit ⇏ *His fast ball is hittable
    d. This bar can be bent ⇏ *This bar is bendable
    e. This match can be lit ⇏ *This match is lightable
    f. The bat can be swung ⇏ *This bat is swingable
    g. The lighthouse can be spotted ⇏ *The lighthouse is spottable
and so on.

5.15 Inchoatives

Consider the following sets of sentences:

    1. a. The metal is hard.   (5-7)
       b. The metal hardened. (The metal became hard.)

2. a. The liquid is cool.
   b. The liquid cooled. (The liquid became cool.)
3. a. The gin is frozen.
   b. The gin froze. (The gin became frozen.)
4. a. The iron is liquid.
   b. The iron liquefied. (The iron became liquid.)
5. a. Mary's dress is loose.
   b. Mary's dress loosened. (Mary's dress became loose.)
6. a. The metal is solid.
   b. The metal solidified. (The metal became solid.)
7. a. The window is broken.
   b. The window broke. (The window became broken.)
8. a. The sauce is thick.
   b. The sauce thickened. (The sauce became thick.)
9. a. Harry is sick.
   b. Harry sickened [at the thought of becoming a linguist]. (Harry became sick. . . .)
10. a. The sky is red.
    b. The sky reddened. (The sky became red.)
11. a. The sky is black.
    b. The sky blackened. (The sky became black.)
12. a. The window is open.
    b. The window opened. (The window became open.)

The a and b sentences are transformationally related. And the b sentences are synonymous with the parenthesized *become* sentences. Thus, it would be quite reasonable to expect the b sentences and the *become* sentences to have very similar deep structures, perhaps even identical, up to lexical items. (This need not necessarily be true, but if it were, the synonymy could be easily explained.) Note also that the *become* sentences are in most cases synonymous with sentences in which *come to be* replaces *become*.

1. a. The liquid became cool.   (5-8)
   b. The liquid came to be cool.
2. a. The sky became black.
   b. The sky came to be black.

We will not go so far as to propose that *become* is derived from *come to be*. Since that is not at issue here, we will only mention the possibility. But the relationship seems more than accidental, and it is conceivable that the *become* and *come to be* sentences have similar—if not identical—deep structures. If this is so, and if the *become* sentences have the same deep structure (up to lexical items) as the b sentences of (5-7), then we would have a strange phenomenon to deal with. Note that the *come to be* sentences contain a complement construction. In the deep structure of *The sky came to be black,* the deep structure of *The sky is black* is contained as a complement. But the b sentences of (5-7) look on the surface like simple intransitives; all traces of a complement construction have disappeared.

Let us first consider the *come to be* sentences. Consider the sentences:

    1. He came to be looked upon as a fool.   (5-9)
    2. It came about that he was looked upon as a fool.

It is clear that in 2 the *that* clause is a subject complement that has been shifted to the end of the sentence. Before this shift, 2 has the structure:

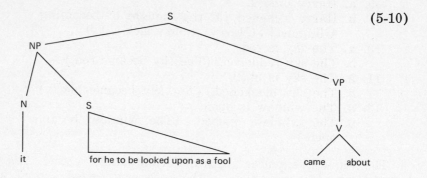

(5-10)

1 has the same structure at some point in its derivation. But 1 undergoes two further rules. *He* substitutes for *it*. And *come* in 1 begins as *come about* and the *about* is deleted by a very general rule. 1 starts out as

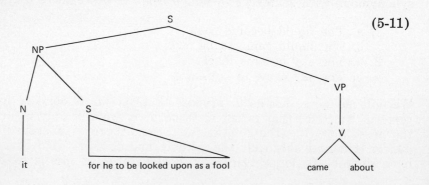

(5-11)

and after extraposition, we get:

(5-12)

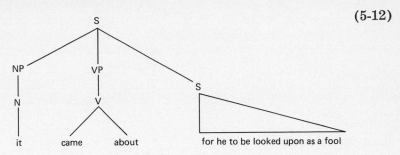

Then *he* substitutes for *it*. (Call the rule IT-SUB.) [See Remark 5-1.] This is the same rule that applies to yield *He happened to be sick* (compare with *It happened that he was sick*) and *He appeared to be sick* (compare with *It appeared that he was sick*).

(5-13)

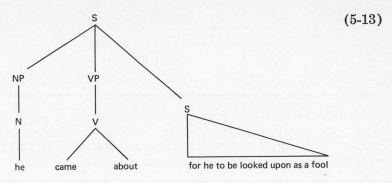

Then the second occurrence of *he* is deleted since it is identical with the first occurrence. (Call the rule ID-NP-DEL.) This is the same rule that produces *I asked to leave* from *I asked for I to leave* (compare with *I asked for John to leave*).

(5-14)

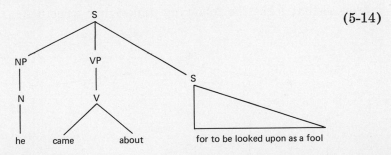

Then *about* is deleted before *for*. The same rule deletes *on* in the derivation of *I decided to go* (compare with *I decided on going*).

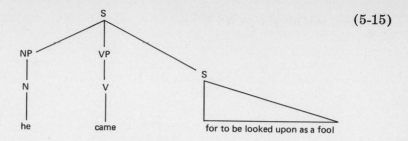

(5-15)

Then *for* is deleted to yield:

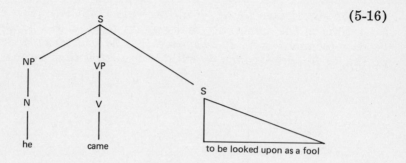

(5-16)

I propose that the *become* sentences work in essentially the same way, except that they undergo a further (minor) rule that deletes *to be*. And I propose that the *get* sentences of (5-17) work in the same way as the *become* sentences.

1. a. The sauce became thick.
   b. The sauce got thick.
2. a. The sky became red.
   b. The sky got red.

(5-17)

I propose that 1 has the following underlying structure:

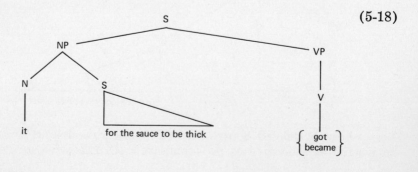

(5-18)

The sauce thickened would have the same deep structure, except that instead of containing a real verb, such as *become* or *get*, it would contain a pro-verb with the same meaning. (We will call this the inchoative pro-verb.) [See Remark 5-2.] *The sauce thickened* would start out as [see Remark 5-3]:

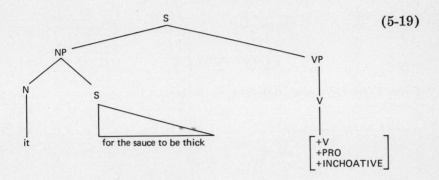

(5-19)

After extraposition, we get:

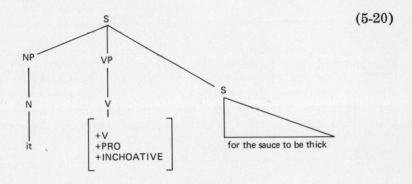

(5-20)

IT-SUB then yields:

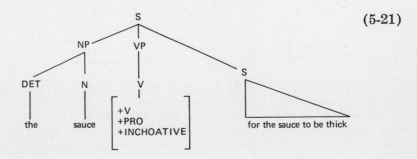

(5-21)

Then ID-NP-SUB:

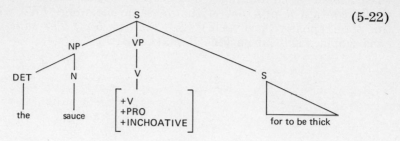

(5-22)

Then FOR-DEL and deletion of *to be:*

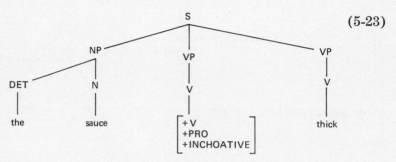

(5-23)

At this point, a rule applies that substitutes *thick* for the inchoative pro-verb [see Remark 5-4]. (We will call this rule INCHOATIVE. It is not clear whether INCHOATIVE deletes *to be* or whether these have not yet been "spelled out" at this point in the derivation.) A later spelling rule will place the ending *-en* on *thick.* Note that INCHOATIVE completely wipes out the structure of the complement, and the derived structure contains no embedded S:

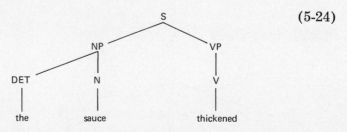

(5-24)

The advantages of this analysis are that we can postulate a single deep structure for the *become, get,* and inchoative sentences at the cost of only one new rule—INCHOATIVE. One bonus that this analysis yields is that it also provides for the analysis of a hitherto mysterious construction—the reflexive inchoative. Consider the following sentences:

1. a. John got hurt when he fell down. (5-25)
   b. John hurt himself when he fell down.
   c. John hurt himself by hitting himself on the head with a hammer.
2. a. John got injured when he fell down.
   b. John injured himself when he fell down.
   c. John injured himself by hitting himself on the head with a hammer.
3. a. John got dirty when he fell down.
   b. John dirtied himself when he fell down.
   c. John dirtied himself by smearing himself with paint.

The a and b sentences are synonymous and have an inchoative sense. They show no sense of agency on John's part. John acts as an agent only in the c sentences, where he inflicts injury upon himself and applies dirt to himself. It would be natural to expect the reflexive to show up in the c sentences, but it is a mystery why it shows up in the b sentences, which, one would guess, have deep structures very much like those of the a sentences.

We can account for the presence of the reflexive in the following way. Assume the b sentences have underlying structures like that of (5-19). That is,

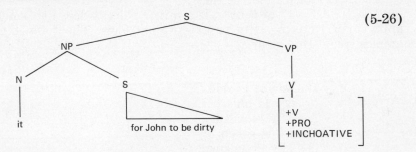

(5-26)

After extraposition and IT-SUB, we get

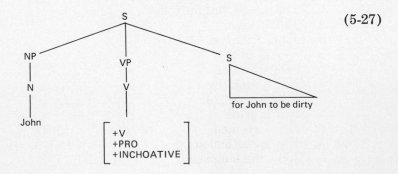

(5-27)

At this point ID-NP-DEL does not take place. We assume that *dirty*, *hurt*, and *injure* are simple exceptions to this rule. IN-CHOATIVE then applies and we get:

(5-28)

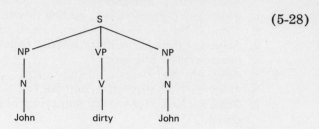

Which becomes *John dirtied himself*, by the reflexive transformation.

Although such constructions are very rare in English and occur only in exceptional cases, they are common in other Indo-European languages. Such reflexive constructions are the normal way of forming the inchoative in Spanish, French, and Russian. One premature guess as to how this comes about (without there being a great number of exceptions in each language) is that in these languages the analogue of INCHOATIVE precedes ID-NP-DEL, and the latter does not apply in these cases since its structural description cannot be met.

INCHOATIVE, of course, is a minor rule. It does not generally apply to adjectives—only to exceptional ones. The following examples make this clear.

1. a. The metal is cold.   (5-29)
   b. *The metal colded.
2. a. The sky is blue.
   b. *The sky bluened.
3. a. The sky is green.
   b. *The sky greenened.
4. a. John is fat.
   b. *John fattened.
5. a. The losses were minimal.
   b. *The losses minimized.
6. a. John is rich.
   b. *John richened.
7. a. John is tall.
   b. *John tallened.
8. a. John is healthy.
   b. *John healthied.
9. a. John is wise.
   b. *John wisened.
10. a. John is meticulous.
    b. *John meticuloused.

5.16 Causatives

Consider the following sentences:

1. a. The metal hardened. (5-30)
   b. John hardened the metal.
   c. John brought it about that the metal hardened.
2. a. The liquid cooled.
   b. John cooled the liquid.
   c. John brought it about that the liquid cooled.
3. a. Mary's dress loosened.
   b. John loosened Mary's dress.
   c. John brought it about that Mary's dress loosened.
4. a. The metal solidified.
   b. John solidified the metal.
   c. John brought it about that the metal solidified.
5. a. The window broke.
   b. John broke the window.
   c. John brought it about that the window broke.
6. a. The sauce thickened.
   b. John thickened the sauce.
   c. John brought it about that the sauce thickened.
7. a. The door opened.
   b. John opened the door.
   c. John brought it about that the door opened.

The a and b sentences are transformationally related, and the b sentences are synonymous with the c sentences. However, the b and c sentences are each ambiguous, and for that reason the synonymy is not always apparent. Consider 7.b and 7.c. Most people, on first glance, would say that 7.b entails direct action, as in:

John opened the door by turning the doorknob. (5-31)

However 7.b can also indicate indirect action, as in:

John opened the door by increasing the air pressure (5-32) in the room to 200 atmospheres.

7.c is, at first glance, usually considered as indicating indirect action, as in:

John brought it about that the door opened by in- (5-33) creasing the air pressure in the room.

However, 7.c may also indicate direct action, as in:

> By turning the doorknob, John brought it about that   (5-34)
> the door opened.

The verbs *bring about* and *cause* both indicate causation and both are ambiguous in the above sense, as are all of the b sentences of (5-30).

Note that in (5-30), we have a phenomenon similar to what we found in the case of inchoative sentences. The b and c sentences, being synonymous, would be likely candidates for having deep structures which are identical up to lexical items. However, the c sentences contain complement constructions; indeed, the deep structure of each c sentence would contain as a complement the deep structure of its corresponding a sentence. The b sentences, on the other hand, look superficially like simple transitive sentences, and on the surface contain no trace of a complement.

I propose the b sentences (which we will call CAUSATIVES) have the same deep structures as the c sentences, except that they have a causative pro-verb, where the c sentences have the verb *bring about*. Thus, *John thickened the sauce* would have the following underlying structure (ignoring the underlying structure of *The sauce thickened,* which we discussed above):

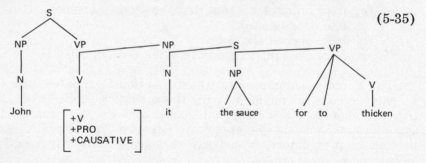

(5-35)

After IT-DEL, a transformation, which we will call CAUSATIVE, will substitute *thicken* for the causative pro-verb. When the verb of the embedded sentence is deleted in the process of substitution, the nodes VP and S are also deleted, and no trace of the complement is left.

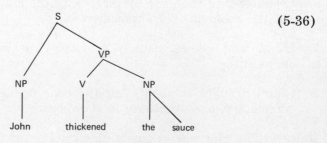

(5-36)

Note that inchoative sentences cannot be derived from subjectless causatives, as has been proposed by Barbara Hall [1965]. If they could be so derived, then any adverbial that could occur with a causative sentence could also occur with its corresponding inchoative. This is not true, particularly in the case of manner adverbials. For example,

1. John broke the window cleverly.   (5-37)
2. *The window broke cleverly.

Note also that according to our analyses of the inchoative and causative, *the sauce* bears the same relation to *thick* in all of the sentences:

1. The sauce is thick.   (5-38)
2. The sauce thickened.
3. John thickened the sauce.

The deep structure for 3 would contain the deep structure for both of the former sentences:

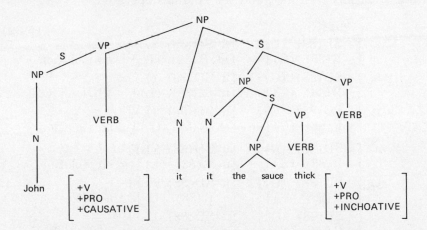

Note that CAUSATIVE operates on inchoative verbs—usually on the product of the inchoative rule. And CAUSATIVE, like INCHOATIVE, is a minor rule.

5.2 A PARTIAL FORMALISM FOR MINOR RULES

If we were interested only in generating the fully grammatical sentences of a language, we could account for exceptions of this sort by use of our interpretation of the Chomsky-Halle conventions [see Section 2.2] for handling minor rules. Since we are interested also in generating the partially grammatical sentences and marking them as such, we will need to employ more apparatus.

There is a clear sense in which minor rules work in just the opposite way from the way in which major rules work. Major rules apply to all regular cases, but not to exceptions. Minor rules do not apply to regular cases, and apply only to exceptions. Compare the table of (5-39) to that of (3-2). Note that wherever there is a *u* for an R feature in (3-2), there is an *m* in (5-39). And wherever there is an *m* in (3-2), there is a *u* in (5-39). This suggests that there is a very simple relation between major and minor rules, namely, in minor rules the polarity of markings is reversed: *u*'s act like *m*'s and *m*'s act like *u*'s.

Assume that Rule 88 is a minor rule. Sentence 1 in (5-39) contains exceptional lexical items: the rule must apply if the structural description is met. 2 contains ordinary lexical items: the minor rule must not operate on them. This table defines all the possibilities that can occur when a minor rule is in the grammar. In a, the structural description for Rule 88 has not been met, and of course the rule has not operated. In b, the structural description has been met, but the rule has not operated. In c, the structural description has been met, and the rule has operated.

(5-39)

1. a. [—SD(88) (G)]   [u SD(88) (L)]
      [—R(88) (G)]   [m R(88) (L)]   no violation

   b. [+SD(88) (G)]   [u SD(88) (L)]
      [—R(88) (G)]   [m R(88) (L)]   VIOLATION

   c. [+SD(88) (G)]   [u SD(88) (L)]
      [+R(88) (G)]   [m R(88) (L)]   no violation

2. a. [—SD(88) (G)]   [u SD(88) (L)]
      [—R(88) (G)]   [u R(88) (L)]   no violation

   b. [+SD(88) (G)]   [u SD(88) (L)]
      [—R(88) (G)]   [u R(88) (L)]   no violation

   c. [+SD(88) (G)]   [u SD(88) (L)]
      [+R(88) (G)]   [u R(88) (L)]   VIOLATION

Since Rule 88 applies to exceptional (marked) lexical items, if the structural description has been met, we get a violation in 1.b since the rule has not applied when it should have. Since Rule 88 may not apply to normal (unmarked) lexical items, we get a violation in case 2.c since it operated when it should not have.

Since minor rules differ from major rules only in that the polarity of markings is reversed for them, we need not set up an entirely new set of metarules to map *m*'s and *u*'s into pluses and minuses. Instead, we need only introduce rules that change *m*'s to

u's and u's to m's in rule features that correspond to minor rules. Then minor rules can be treated as major rules, and we can apply the metarules of (3-3), (3-4), and (3-5) to yield the correct results.

For each minor rule of a language, we will have a rule of the form:

$$[\gamma \ R(i) \ (L)] \rightarrow [\sim \gamma \ R(i) \ (L)], \qquad (5\text{-}40)$$

where $\gamma = u$ or m
$\sim u = m$
$\sim m = u$
R(i) is the minor rule in question.

Thus the rule

$$[\gamma \ R(88) \ (L)] \rightarrow [\sim \gamma \ R(88) \ (L)] \qquad (5\text{-}41)$$

will map each of the cases indicated on the chart of (5-39) into the corresponding cases on the chart of (3-2), with 88 substituting for 89. The Metarules 1, 3, and 5 of (3-3), (3-4), and (3-5) will map those cases into the corresponding cases on the chart of (3-6), again with 88 substituting for 89. This will yield the correct result in each case.

Rules of the form (5-40) are roughly equivalent to Chomsky-Halle rules of the form (2-4) with a null environment; namely, the special Chomsky-Halle rules which, under our interpretation of them, can indicate when a following rule is minor. Rules like (5-40) are language-particular rules, whose symbols would be counted in an evaluation procedure—which would mean that grammars with more minor rules would be valued less highly. However, rules of the form (5-40) have no direct linguistic interpretation. If one does not consider these rules together with Metarules 1, 3, and 5, it is not clear what it means to change an m into a u or a u into an m.

Rules like (5-40) make sense only when combined with Metarules 1, 3, and 5. Since this is the case, it might be wise to employ an equivalent formalism in which rules of the form (5-40) are considered as metarules. In the formalism, a grammar may contain a list of minor rules. Since each rule of the form of (5-40) contains the same number of symbols (say that the number is n), our evaluation procedure will evaluate the list by considering each rule number on the list to count n symbols. Our linguistic theory would then include a mechanical procedure that takes the list of minor rules as input and produces a sequence of metarules of the form of (5-40). For instance, if 88 were on such a list, the mechanical procedure would produce (5-41) as a metarule. These metarules would, of course, apply before Metarules 1, 3, and 5.

5.3 PARTLY MINOR RULES

There not only exist minor rules in English, but there also exist rules that are major for one subcategory of lexical items and minor for another. Consider WH-DEL [see Section A.4]. WH-DEL applies to almost all adjectives, with a few exceptions, such as *ready, glad, sorry,* and so on.

(5-42)

WH-DEL   ADJ-SHIFT

a. The boy who is ready ⇒ *the boy ready ⇒ *the ready boy
b. The boy who is glad ⇒ *the boy glad ⇒ *the glad boy
c. The boy who is sorry ⇒ *the boy sorry ⇒ *the sorry boy
d. The boy who is content ⇒ *the boy content ⇒ *the content boy

These adjectives seem to be exceptions to WH-DEL, not to ADJ-SHIFT, otherwise the intermediate expressions in (5-42) would be grammatical.

There are also a number of verbs that can undergo WH-DEL. For example, *beat, murder, control, capture,* and so forth.

(5-43)

a. The man who was beaten ⇒ the man beaten ⇒ the beaten man
b. The man who was murdered ⇒ the man murdered ⇒ the murdered man
c. The experiment which was controlled ⇒ the experiment controlled ⇒ the controlled experiment
d. The bird that was captured ⇒ the bird captured ⇒ the captured bird

But the great bulk of verbs cannot undergo WH-DEL:

(5-44)

a. The man who was shot ⇒ *the man shot ⇒ *the shot man
b. The boy who was hit ⇒ *the boy hit ⇒ *the hit boy
c. The store that was robbed ⇒ *the store robbed ⇒ *the robbed store
d. The man who was killed ⇒ *the man killed ⇒ *the killed man
e. The food that was eaten ⇒ *the food eaten ⇒ *the eaten food
f. The bird that was caught ⇒ *the bird caught ⇒ *the caught bird
g. The horse that was tied ⇒ *the horse tied ⇒ the tied horse

Thus, WH-DEL is a rule that is major for adjectives and minor for verbs. That is, WH-DEL is major for [+V, +ADJECTIVAL] and minor for [+V, −ADJECTIVAL]. (This analysis is somewhat incorrect. [See Remark 8-1.])

Another rule of the same sort is object deletion [OBJ-DEL; see Section A.7]. A number of transitive verbs allow unspecified objects to be deleted.

a. John is eating something ⇒ John is eating   (5-45)
b. John is drinking something ⇒ John is drinking
c. John is writing something ⇒ John is writing

However, most transitive verbs cannot delete unspecified objects.

                                                    (5-46)

a. John is robbing something ⇏ *John is robbing
b. John is touching something ⇏ *John is touching
c. John is explaining something ⇏ *John is explaining
d. John is wearing something ⇏ *John is wearing
e. John is controlling something ⇏ *John is controlling

Adjectives, on the other hand, normally may delete unspecified (derived) objects.

a. Skiing is beneficial to people ⇒ Skiing is beneficial   (5-47)
b. His remark was suggestive of something ⇒ His remark was suggestive
c. That was amusing to someone ⇒ That was amusing
d. John was wary of someone ⇒ John was wary
e. John was brutal to someone ⇒ John was brutal
f. Harry was afraid of something ⇒ Harry was afraid
g. Cigarettes are harmful to people ⇒ Cigarettes are harmful
h. John was sorry about something ⇒ John was sorry

However, there are a few exceptional adjectives that cannot delete unspecified objects.

a. John is fond of something ⇏ *John is fond   (5-48)
b. His action was equivalent to something ⇏ *His action was equivalent
c. John was cognizant of something ⇏ *John was cognizant
d. Bill was desirous of something ⇏ *Bill was desirous

Thus, OBJ-DEL is major for adjectives and minor for verbs.

5.4 A PARTIAL FORMALISM FOR PARTLY MINOR RULES

We can handle situations of this sort by using rules of the form of
(5-40) with environment statements. For instance, the cases in the
previous section might be handled by the rules:

a. $[\gamma \ R[\text{WH-DEL}]] \rightarrow [\sim \gamma \ R[\text{WH-DEL}]]/$ (5-49)
$\quad [+V, \ -\text{ADJECTIVAL},]$
b. $[\gamma \ R[\text{OBJ-DEL}]] \rightarrow [\sim \gamma \ R[\text{OBJ-DEL}]]/$
$\quad [+V, \ -\text{ADJECTIVAL},]$

a says that R (WH-DEL) is minor for verbs; b says that R (OBJ-
DEL) is minor for verbs.

We can extend our formalism in which minor rules are given
in a list that is converted into a sequence of metarules in the following way: Instead of having a simple list of rule names (or
numbers), we will have a list of ordered pairs, the first member
of which will be a rule name, the second member of which will
be an environment statement. Given these, our revised mechanical
procedure will convert list entries like WH-DEL; [+V, —AD-
JECTIVAL, __] and OBJ-DEL; [+V, —ADJECTIVAL, __] into
metarules such as (5-49).

Note that (5-49) is of the same form as (C-8) and (C-17).
Thus, using our notion of markedness we have found cases involving rule features which are parallel to cases involving ordinary
syntactic features (C-17) and to cases involving phonological features (C-8).

6 ABSOLUTE EXCEPTIONS

So far we have considered two types of exceptions:

1. a. cases in which an item meeting the structural description of a rule may not undergo the rule
   b. cases in which most items which meet the structural description of a rule must not undergo it, but a few items may

We will now consider two further types:

2. a. cases in which an item must not meet the structural description of some rule
   b. cases in which an item *must* meet the structural description of some rule

We will call 2 "absolute exceptions."

6.1 ITEMS THAT MUST NOT MEET STRUCTURAL DESCRIPTIONS

Consider the following sentences:

1. a. I begged John to go.   (6-1)
   b. I begged to go.
2. a. I implored John to go.
   b. *I implored to go.
   c. *I implored myself to go.
   d. *I implored for me to go.

3. a. I yelled for John to go.
   b. *I yelled to go.
   c. *I yelled for me to go.
   d. *I yelled myself to go.
4. a. I shouted for John to come.
   b. *I shouted to come.
   c. *I shouted for me to come.
   d. *I shouted myself to come.
5. a. I besought John to leave.
   b. *I besought to leave.
   c. *I besought for me to leave.
   d. *I besought myself to leave.
6. a. I bade him go.
   b. *I bade go.
   c. *I bade myself go.
   d. *I bade for me to go.

In 1.b, *beg* has undergone the widespread rule that deletes the subject of an embedding when it is identical to the subject of the matrix sentence (ID-NP-DEL). The other b sentences show, however, that *implore, shout, yell, beseech,* and *bid* may not undergo this rule. If these verbs were simple exceptions that could not undergo ID-NP-DEL when they met its structural description, one would expect the subject of the embedded sentence to appear, even though it was identical to that of the matrix sentence. As the c and d sentences in (6-1) show, this is not the case. The identical embedded subjects may neither appear, nor be deleted. Not only can these verbs not undergo ID-NP-DEL, they *may not even meet its structural description.*

Irreflexive verbs also exemplify this phenomenon [see Remark 6-1]. Consider the following:

1. a. I will meet Bill.   (6-2)
   b. *I will meet myself.
   c. *I will meet me.
2. a. You will follow Bill.
   b. *You will follow yourself.
   c. *You will follow you.
3. a. You will precede Bill.
   b. *You will precede yourself.
   c. *You will precede you.
4. a. I assassinated Harry.
   b. *I assassinated myself.
   c. *I assassinated me.

The b sentences demonstrate that these verbs may not undergo the reflexive transformation. If they were simple exceptions to the reflexive, we would expect the c sentences to occur. They do not. In essence, these verbs may not have an object which is identical to their subject. A natural way to express this is to say that they may not meet the structural description of the reflexive transformation.

6.2 ITEMS THAT MUST MEET STRUCTURAL DESCRIPTIONS

It is usually the case that when a structural description of a rule is not met, no violation of the rule is possible. For example, consider:

1. *I wanted for me to go.   (6-3)
2. I wanted to go.
3. I wanted for John to go.
4. I wanted John to go.

In sentence 1 the matrix and embedded subjects are identical, and the SD of ID-NP-DEL is met. If ID-NP-DEL does not operate, we get a violation as in sentence 1. If it does operate, we get 2 as a grammatical sentence. If the SD of ID-NP-DEL is not met, as in sentence 3 then, of course, the rule need not operate, and so we get the grammatical sentences of 3 and 4. This is the usual situation.

However, the sentences of (6-4) do not work this way.

1. a. John refrained from doing that.   (6-4)
   b. *John refrained from Bill's doing that.
2. a. John tried escaping.
   b. *John tried Bill's escaping.
   c. *John tried Bill escaping.
3. a. John was clever in leaving early.
   b. *John was clever in Bill's leaving early.
4. a. John was wise in cornering the market on schmoos.
   b. *John was wise in Bill's cornering the market on schmoos.

In each of the a sentences, the embedded subject has been deleted, since it was identical to the matrix subject. But if, as in the b sentences, the matrix subject is not identical to the embedded subject, that is, if the SD of ID-NP-DEL is not met, then no grammatical sentence can result. Those VERBS *must meet the structural description of* ID-NP-DEL.

Necessarily reflexive verbs may be looked upon as having to

meet the structural description of the reflexive transformation. For example,

(6-5)

1. a. John behaved himself.
    b. *John behaved Harry.
2. a. John prided himself on being faster than a speeding bullet.
    b. *John prided Bill on being faster than a speeding bullet.

(Note that if one adopted such an analysis of these reflexives, one would have to explain why there is no reflexive in the nominalizations of these verbs. We get *John's behavior* and *John's pride in being faster than a speeding bullet* instead of **John's behavior of himself* and **John's pride in himself in being faster than a speeding bullet*. At this time we can offer no well-motivated explanation of this phenomenon. Of course, one can always describe the facts by postulating a minor rule which deletes the reflexive object in only these verbs. But this is at least as bad as considering the verbs to be intransitive and postulating a minor rule applying only to these verbs that places a copy of the subject in the object position, providing that the verbs are not nominalized.)

6.3   A PARTIAL FORMALISM FOR ABSOLUTE EXCEPTIONS

So far, we have seen that verbs exist that must meet the SD of some rule, or that must not meet the SD of some rule. Before going on to consider some further cases of these phenomena, we will provide a formalism for handling them.

We will employ the SD features which we defined in Section 6.2.

6.31   Positive Absolute Exceptions

As we saw in Section 6.2, *attempt* is an exception in a way that *want* is not. *Attempt* must meet the SD of ID-NP-DEL, whereas *want* need not do so. That is, *attempt* is nonnormal, while *want* is a normal case. Thus, we will consider *attempt* to be marked with respect to the SD feature of ID-NP-DEL, while *want* will be unmarked. Note that *attempt* is unmarked for the rule feature of ID-NP-DEL. *Attempt* yields a violation if it does not meet the SD of ID-NP-DEL. If, however, it does meet that SD, then *attempt* works like a normal word from that point on: if the rule does not operate, we get a violation (*John attempted for John to go*); if the rule operates, we do not get a violation (*John attempted to go*).

These possibilities are represented as follows:

(6-6)

a. [−SD(ID-NP-DEL) (G)]   [m SD(ID-NP-DEL) (L)]
   [−R(ID-NP-DEL) (G)]   [u R(ID-NP-DEL) (L)]
               VIOLATION

b. [+SD(ID-NP-DEL) (G)]   [m SD(ID-NP-DEL) (L)]
   [−R(ID-NP-DEL) (G)]   [u R(ID-NP-DEL) (L)]
               VIOLATION

c. [+SD(ID-NP-DEL) (G)]   [m SD(ID-NP-DEL) (L)]
   [+R(ID-NP-DEL) (G)]   [u R(ID-NP-DEL) (L)]
               no violation

Note that in cases like *attempt* we fail to get a violation only in case c, where the SD is met *and* the rule has operated. We can account for all these possibilities by adding the following metarule to those of (3-3), (3-4), and (3-5):

Metarule 4: For all rules *i*,   (6-7)
   [m SD(i) (L)] → [+SD(i) (L)]

Metarule 4, applied with Metarule 5 [see (3-5)], will map the lexical features of (6-6) into those of (6-8):

(6-8)

a. [−SD (ID-NP-DEL) (G)]   [+SD(ID-NP-DEL) (L)]
   [−R(ID-NP-DEL) (G)]   [+R(ID-NP-DEL) (L)]
               VIOLATION

b. [+SD(ID-NP-DEL) (G)]   [+SD(ID-NP-DEL) (L)]
   [−R(ID-NP-DEL) (G)]   [+R(ID-NP-DEL) (L)]
               VIOLATION

c. [+SD(ID-NP-DEL) (G)]   [+SD(ID-NP-DEL) (L)]
   [+R(ID-NP-DEL) (G)]   [+R(ID-NP-DEL) (L)]
               no violation

6.32 Negative Absolute Exceptions

Verbs like *implore* and *beseech* seem to be even less "normal" than verbs like *attempt* that are marked for the SD feature of some rule. In some sense, verbs that may not meet the SD of some rule seem even more exceptional than those that must do so. To account for this, we will hypothesize that such verbs are marked for *both* the SD feature *and* the R feature of the rule in question. Note that it is completely reasonable to hypothesize that the R feature is marked for such verbs. By Metarule 1 [see (3-3)], a marked R feature will always be interpreted as a minus R feature, which means that the rule in question should never operate on an item represented in that fashion. This is correct for these cases, since an item that may not meet the SD of a rule may not undergo that rule. Note that the latter is an empirical, not a logical, fact. It is logically possible that there could exist exceptions of such a type that they produced violations if they met the SD of a rule but did not undergo the rule, and did not produce violations if they either did not meet the SD or *both* met the SD and underwent the rule. We have never found any such cases, and the system that we have set up so far incorporates the claim that they do not exist [see Metarule 5 (3-5)].

The possibilities for verbs that may not meet the SD of some rule are represented in (6-9). Let Rule 90 be the rule in question.

(6-9)

a. [−SD(90) (G)]   [m SD(90) (L)]   no violation
   [−R(90) (G)]   [m R(90) (L)]

b. [+SD(90) (G)]   [m SD(90) (L)]   VIOLATION
   [−R(90) (G)]   [m R(90) (L)]

c. [+SD(90) (G)]   [m SD(90) (L)]   VIOLATION
   [+R(90) (G)]   [m R(90) (L)]

To yield the correct results, the lexical features of (6-9) would have to be mapped into those of (6-10).

(6-10)

a. [−SD(90) (G)]   [−SD(90) (L)]   no violation
   [−R(90) (G)]   [−R(90) (L)]

b. [+SD(90) (G)]   [−SD(90) (L)]   VIOLATION
   [−R(90) (G)]   [−R(90) (L)]

c. [+SD(90) (G)]   [−SD(90) (L)]   VIOLATION
   [+R(90) (G)]   [−R(90) (L)]

Our present metarules will not perform this mapping correctly. In particular, Metarule 4 will incorrectly map the marked SD features into plus SD features. To circumvent this we will add the following metarule:

Metarule 2: for all rules i,   (6-11)

[m SD (i) (L)] → [−SD(i) (L)]/ $\boxed{\text{−R (i) (L)}}$

The environment for this metarule will be produced by Metarule

1. Metarules 1 through 5 will now yield the correct results for all the cases we have considered so far.

For the convenience of the reader we include the entire list.

For all rules i,   (6-12)

Metarule 1.
[m R(i) (L)] → [−R(i) (L)]

Metarule 2.
[m SD(i) (L)] → [−SD(i) (L)]/ $\boxed{\begin{array}{cc} −R(i) & (L) \end{array}}$

Metarule 3.
[u SD(i) (L)] → [α SD(i) (L)]/ $\boxed{\begin{array}{cc} α\ SD(i) & (G) \end{array}}$

Metarule 4.
[m SD(i) (L)] → [+SD(i) (L)]

Metarule 5.
[u R(i) (L)] → [α R(i) (L)]/ $\boxed{\begin{array}{cc} α\ SD(i) & (L) \end{array}}$

6.33 Absolute Exceptions to Minor Rules

There exist cases in which items must meet the structural description not of a major rule, but of a minor rule. Consider *legible* as opposed to *readable*. As we pointed out in Section 5.14, *readable* is formed by a minor rule which we called ABLE-SUB. *Read*, unlike most verbs, may undergo ABLE-SUB if it meets the SD of that rule. However, *read* need not necessarily meet the SD of ABLE-SUB, and may occur in such sentences as *I read what he wrote*. *Legible* is understood in the same way in which *readable* is understood. However, the verb stem *leg-* may not occur in any sentence of English unless it has undergone ABLE-SUB. This means that *leg-* must both meet the SD of ABLE-SUB and undergo the rule.

Read, as we mentioned above, must be marked for the ABLE-SUB rule feature: that is, it must contain the feature [m R(ABLE-SUB) (L)]. *Leg-* must also contain this feature. However, since it must meet the SD of ABLE-SUB, it must contain the feature [m SD(ABLE-SUB) (L)] as well. That is, it will be marked for *both* the R feature and the SD feature of ABLE-SUB. This is intuitively correct, since *leg-* is clearly less "normal" than is *read*. Note that since ABLE-SUB is a minor rule there will be a metarule that will change [m R(ABLE-SUB) (L)] into [u R(ABLE-SUB) (L)] before Metarules 1 through 5 are applied. Thus, Metarules 1 through 5 will treat *leg-* exactly as they would treat any other item that had to meet the SD of some rule.

So far we have not found any items that must not meet the SD of a minor rule. Since items that must not meet the SD of a major rule are comparatively rare, it is not surprising that we have not found such a case. Indeed, we may never find one. However, if such items should ever turn up, the theory we have set up so far would make a claim about them. According to our theory, such items would have to be represented in the lexicon with a marked SD feature and with an *unmarked* R feature. This would embody the claim that such an item would seem intuitively more "normal" than an item such as *leg-*. We can attempt to rationalize this claim in the following way: Since minor rules normally do not apply, the most exceptional case that one could find with respect to such a rule would be an item to which that rule *always* had to apply, namely, an item that had to meet the SD of that rule. On the other hand, an item that could not meet the SD of a minor rule could therefore not undergo that rule—and in that respect it would be like completely normal items and therefore less "abnormal." Unfortunately, this is not an altogether compelling argument—and even if it were, we should still have to await the discovery of empirical evidence to see whether our claim would stand up.

Note that the unmarked R feature on such items would be mapped into a marked R feature by the metarule corresponding to the minor rule in question, and so would be handled by Metarules 1 through 5 exactly like items that cannot meet the SD of some major rule.

6.4 HYPOTHETICAL LEXICAL ITEMS

So far we have shown that absolute exceptions do exist and we have incorporated into our theory of language devices for handling them. These devices are quite powerful, and it would not be surprising if they could be used to describe phenomena that have previously defied adequate description. Nor would it be surprising if these devices permitted alternate descriptions for phenomena which can be described with some degree of adequacy without such devices.

In the remainder of this chapter we will attempt to use our apparatus for handling absolute exceptions to describe phenomena that so far have been handled without such apparatus. We will try to find empirical justification, as far as is possible for each decision, to use these devices.

6.41 Background

Robert Lees [1960] showed that a large number of English abstract nouns are systematically related to verbs. Some examples are *criticize-criticism, transgress-transgression, annoy-annoyance, move-movement.*

1. a. Frye criticized the book.   (6-13)
   b. Frye's criticism of the book
2. a. John transgressed against society.
   b. John's transgression against society
3. a. The ship moved through the water.
   b. The ship's movement through the water
4. a. Being bothered annoys me.
   b. My annoyance at being bothered

Lees proposed that each of the b noun phrases be derived from the abstract structure underlying its corresponding a sentence. Though Lees's arguments in favor of his proposal are well known and have generally been accepted for some time, we will repeat some of them here so that we can make use of them later.

The a sentences share co-occurrence restrictions with the b noun phrases. Consider the following:

1. a. *The lawnmower criticized the book.   (6-14)
   b. *The lawnmower's criticism of the book
2. a. *The tuba transgressed against society.
   b. *The tuba's transgression against society
3. a. *Intelligence moved through the water.
   b. *Intelligence's movement through the water
4. a. *Being bothered annoyed the floor.
   b. *The floor's annoyance at being bothered
1'. a. *Frye criticized my toenail.
   b. *Frye's criticism of my toenail
2'. a. *John transgressed against the pencil
       sharpener.
   b. *John's transgression against the pencil
       sharpener
3'. a. *The ship moved with deep regret.
   b. *The ship's movement with deep regret
4'. a. *Four liters annoyed me.
   b. *My annoyance at four liters

The restrictions on each of the abstract nouns in the b noun phrases follow from the restrictions on the corresponding verbs in the a sentences. Since contextual restrictions on verbs are needed independently of the way we deal with nouns, we can avoid duplicating these restrictions on nouns by deriving the nouns from their corresponding verbs. The rules of derivation will embody a description of the intuitively felt relationships between the a sentences and the b noun phrases. Such a derivation will also account for the fact that the same grammatical relations appear to be present in the a and b cases. In (6-13), *Frye* and *book* seem to bear the same relations, respectively, to *criticism* as they do to *criticize*. *My* seems to bear the same relation to *annoyance* as *me* does to *annoy.* And we can sensibly make such statements as: *ship* is the subject of *movement* in 3.b of (6-13), in the same sense that *ship* is the subject of *move* in 3.a. Since relations such as "subject of" are defined in terms of simple sentences, not in terms of the internal structure of noun phrases, it appears that such statements can make sense only if the noun phrases are derived from simple sentences, and the abstract nouns are derived from verbs. Thus, we would not list *criticism, annoyance, transgression,* and *movement* in the lexicon at all. Rather we would list only their corresponding verbs, and derive all the occurrences of the nouns from occurrences of the verbs.

As Chomsky pointed out [1957] this solution not only *can* be adopted, but *must* be adopted. Any attempt to define such notions as "subject-of" and "object-of" in terms of the internal structure of noun phrases would fail because of such classic cases as

1. the shooting of the hunters   (6-15)
2. the raising of flowers
3. the growling of lions

Phrase 1 is ambiguous; *the hunters* may be either the subject or object of *shooting*. In 2, *flowers* is understood as the object of *raising*. In 3, *lions* is understood as the subject of *growling*.

Any attempt to define "subject-of" and "object-of" in terms of noun phrase structure would fail even more seriously in the cases of agent and object nominals. Consider the following expressions:

1. a. the rulers of the people of Vietnam   (6-16)
   b. the prisoners of the people of Vietnam
2. a. the boss of the union
   b. the requirements of the union

Ruler and *boss* are understood as subjects of the verbs *to rule* and *to boss* respectively. 1.a is synonymous with *the ones who rule the people of Vietnam.* 2.a is synonymous with *the one who bosses the union.* On the other hand, *prisoners* and *requirements* are understood as the "objects" of *to imprison* and *to require* respectively. 1.b. is synonymous with *those who the people of Vietnam have imprisoned.* 2.b is synonymous with *what the union requires.*

It seems clear, then, that abstract, agent, and object nouns that have corresponding verbs *must* be transformationally derived from those verbs.

6.42 The Basic Argument

It has thus far been assumed by Chomsky, Lees, and all other writers on transformational grammar that an abstract noun can be derived from a verb only if that verb can occur in fully grammatical sentences of the language in question. All other abstract nouns, they assume, must be listed as nouns in the lexicon. Yet, it very often happens that one can find two abstract nouns that are used and understood in virtually the same way, but whereas one has a corresponding verb, the other has none. The consequence is that in the current theory of transformational grammar the former would not be listed in the lexicon, but would be derived from its corresponding verb, while the latter would be listed as a noun in the lexicon. Consider the following example:

1. a. I was shocked by John's transgression against   (6-17)
   society.
   b. I was shocked by China's aggression against
   India.
2. a. John transgressed against society.
   b. *China aggressed against India.

The same would be true for the corresponding agent nouns.

1. a. John was a transgressor.   (6-18)
   b. China was the aggressor.

Transgression and *transgressor* would not be listed in the lexicon, but would be derived from *transgress*. The relationship among the three words would be represented in this way. *Aggression* and *aggressor* would both have to be listed as in the lexicon as nouns —and as separate lexical items at that—since there is no occurring verb *to aggress*. Although *aggression* seems related to *aggressor* in the same way as *transgression* is related to *transgressor,* this relationship would go unexpressed. This seems to be a defect in the present theory of transformational grammar, and we propose that it can be corrected only by allowing hypothetical, but non-occurring, items to be represented in the lexicon. In the example under consideration we would claim that a grammar of English could achieve descriptive adequacy only if it included the hypothetical verb *to aggress*. Of course, *aggress* would have to be listed with appropriate restrictions in order to keep *China is aggressing against India* and *I don't like China to aggress against India* from being generated.

We propose that the proper way to restrict the occurrence of lexical items such as *aggress* is by the use of structural description features. *Aggress* can be looked upon as absolute exception. If we consider only *aggression* and not *aggressor* for the moment, we can look upon *aggress* as an item which can never occur in a grammatical sentence of English without undergoing nominalization. This is, *aggress* can occur in a grammatical sentence of English only if it has met the structural description of the nominalization transformation and undergone that rule. In this sense it can be looked at as a positive absolute exception, such as those discussed in Section 6.2. We would represent *aggress* in the lexicon with the features:

$$
\begin{bmatrix}
\text{m SD(NOM) (L)} \\
\text{u R(NOM) (L)} \\
\qquad aggress
\end{bmatrix}
$$

Suppose such a lexical item occurred in a derivation in which the structural description of the nominalization transformation was not met. Its complex symbol would contain:

$$
\begin{bmatrix}
-\text{SD(NOM) (G)} & \quad \text{m SD(NOM) (L)} \\
-\text{R(NOM) (G)} \quad , & \quad \text{u R(NOM) (L)} \\
& \qquad aggress
\end{bmatrix}
\qquad (6\text{-}19)
$$

Metarules 1 through 5 would map this into:

$$
\begin{bmatrix}
-\text{SD(NOM) (G)} & \quad +\text{SD(NOM) (L)} \\
-\text{R(NOM) (G)} \quad , & \quad +\text{R(NOM) (L)} \\
& \qquad aggress
\end{bmatrix}
\qquad (6\text{-}20)
$$

and a violation would result.

If *aggress* occurred in a derivation in which the structural description of the nominalization transformation was met but the rule did not operate, we would get:

$$
\begin{bmatrix}
+\text{SD(NOM) (G)} & \quad \text{m SD(NOM) (L)} \\
-\text{R(NOM) (G)} \quad , & \quad \text{u R(NOM) (L)} \\
& \qquad aggress
\end{bmatrix}
\qquad (6\text{-}21)
$$

This would be mapped into:

$$
\begin{bmatrix}
+\text{SD(NOM) (G)} & \quad +\text{SD(NOM) (L)} \\
-\text{R(NOM) (G)} \quad , & \quad +\text{R(NOM) (L)} \\
& \qquad aggress
\end{bmatrix}
\qquad (6\text{-}22)
$$

This also yields a violation.

On the other hand, if *aggress* both met the SD of the nominalization transformation and underwent the rule, we would get the following situation:

$$
\begin{bmatrix}
\text{+SD(NOM) (G)} & \text{m SD(NOM) (L)} \\
\text{+R(NOM) (G)} & \text{,} & \text{u SD(NOM) (L)} \\
& \textit{aggress}
\end{bmatrix}
\qquad (6\text{-}23)
$$

This would be mapped into:

$$
\begin{bmatrix}
\text{+SD(NOM) (G)} & \text{+SD(NOM) (L)} \\
\text{+R(NOM) (G)} & \text{,} & \text{+R(NOM) (L)} \\
& \textit{aggress}
\end{bmatrix}
\qquad (6\text{-}24)
$$

and there would be no violation. Thus we can handle cases of this sort without setting up special arbitrary features. Instead, we can use the independently motivated descriptive apparatus of SD features.

In the succeeding sections we will attempt to provide syntactic motivation for setting up other hypothetical lexical items.

6.43 Abstract Nouns

English has a great number of abstract nouns like *aggression,* which we will claim must be derived from hypothetical verbs. Although these verbs do not occur in fully grammatical sentences of English, they do occur in sentences which are very nearly grammatical. We will use this fact, in conjunction with the arguments of Section 6.41, to support our claim.

The following examples contain hypothetical verb-abstract noun pairs, which are very similar to the pairs of (6-13):

    1. a.   *Frye critiqued the book.   (6-25)
       b.   Frye's critique of the book
    2. a.   *China aggressed against India.
       b.   China's aggression against India
    3. a.   *The ship moted through the water.
       b.   The ship's motion through the water
    4. a.   *Being bothered consternated me.
      a'.   *Being bothered consterned me.
       b.   My consternation at being bothered

Compare these expressions with those of (6-13). Note that although the a sentences are not fully grammatical, we can understand them easily and make grammatical judgments about them. What is the subject of 1.a? Obviously *Frye.* What is the object of 1.a? Obviously *the book.* What is the subject of 2.a? Obviously *China.* Which is better: *Frye critiqued the book* or *My toenail critiqued the book?* Obviously the former. Which is better: *Frye critiqued the book* or *Sincerity critiqued the book?* Again the former. *Frye critiqued the book* or *Frye critiqued that Bill went there?* The former once more. Note that all of these judgments correspond to our judgments of the ungrammaticality of *My toenail's critique of the book, Sincerity's critique of the book,* and *Frye's critique that Bill went there.* Even though the verb *to consternate* (or *to constern*) does not exist, people who know what *consternation* means and who know how to use it will also understand *consternate* (or *constern*), know how to use it, and make grammatical judgments about it. For example, they will know that *me* bears the same relation to *consternate* in the nonsentence 4.a as *my* bears to *consternation* in 4.b. And they will know that *The robbery consternated me* is more grammatical than *I consternated the robbery,* and they will know that this fact corresponds to the fact that *my consternation at the robbery* is grammatical whereas *the robbery's consternation at me* is not.

In the following examples, we will use a ** to indicate sentences that are less grammatical than those marked with a * in (6-25). Note that the asterisked a sentences of (6-25) bear the same relation to the fully grammatical b noun phrases of (6-25) as the a sentences of (6-13) bear to the b noun phrases of (6-13). We can see in the following example that the hypothetical verbs of the (6-25) a sentences share co-occurrence restrictions with abstract nouns of (6-25) b noun phrases.

1. a. **The lawnmower critiqued the book.   (6-26)
   b. *The lawnmower's critique of the book
2. a. **The tuba aggressed against India.
   b. *The tuba's aggression against India
3. a. **Intelligence moted through the water.
   b. *Intelligence's motion through the water
4. a. **Being bothered conternated the floor.
   b. *The floor's conternation at being bothered
1'. a. **Frye critiqued my toenail.
   b. *Frye's critique of my toenail
2'. a. **China aggressed against the pencil
         sharpener.
   b. *China's aggression against the pencil
         sharpener
3'. a. **The ship moved with deep regret.
   b. *The ship's motion with deep regret
4'. a. **Four liters consternated me.
   b. *My consternation at four liters

As in (6-25), the noun phrases of b are more grammatical than the sentences of a; the violation of selectional restrictions has lowered the grammaticality of each in the same way, just as in (6-13). If we list *critique, aggress, move,* and *consternate* as hypothetical verbs (absolute exceptions) in the lexicon and derive the b noun phrases from abstract structures underlying the a sentences, then all of the facts that we have mentioned so far will be automatically accounted for. If, however, we list only abstract nouns in the lexicon, it is difficult to see how any of these facts can be accounted for. Moreover, if we list the abstract nouns in the lexicon, we will have to allow them to be subcategorized in the same way in which verbs can be subcategorized. And the difficulty of defining grammatical relations within noun phrases arises again.

Compare the grammatical relations in the b noun phrases of (6-25) with those of (6-13). *Frye* seems to bear the same relation to *critique* as to *criticism. Book* seems to bear the same relation to *critique* as to *criticism. Ship* seems to bear the same relation to *movement* as it does to *motion. Through the water* seems to bear the same relation to *movement* as to *motion,* and so on. These facts can be accounted for automatically if the b noun phrases of (6-25) are derived from the a sentences of (6-25). If we do not choose this alternative, then we cannot account for our intuitions about grammatical relations in the partially grammatical a sentences of (6-25), and we would face the hopeless task of defining grammatical relations in terms of the internal structure of noun phrases. For instance, in

1. the critique of the book   (6-27)
2. the motion of the ship

we must be able to tell that *book* is the object of *critique,* but that *ship* is the subject of *motion.* Thus, a natural way to account for all these facts—and the only way that has been suggested thus far —would be to derive abstract nouns such as those in the b phrases of (6-23) from hypothetical verbs.

We leave open the question as to whether all abstract nouns which are not correlated with any actually occurring verbs are to be derived from hypothetical verbs. It appears that where the above arguments can be made, where we have clear intuitions about the grammatical properties of nonoccurring verbs, we must hypothesize those verbs simply to account for the facts. It is our guess that this will be true for an overwhelming number of abstract nouns. It would not be surprising if all abstract nouns turned out to be derived from verbs (or adjectives)—hypothetical or otherwise.

6.44 Agent Nouns

There are a large number of agent nouns that do not correspond to existing verbs and that are understood in the same way as agent nouns that are transformationally derived from existing verbs. *Aggressor* in Section 6.42 is one example. The following are other examples:

A. 1. a. John is a robber.   (6-28)
       b. John is a thief.
    2. a. John robs things.
       b. *John thieves things. (compare *thievery*)

B. 1. a. Harry is the ruler of Liechtenstein.
       b. Harry is the king of Liechtenstein.
    2. a. Harry rules Liechtenstein.
       b. *Harry kings Liechtenstein.

C. 1. a. John is a transgressor.
       b. China was the aggressor.
    2. a. John transgressed against society.
       b. *China aggressed against India.

D. 1. a. John is a painter.
       b. John is a plumber.
    2. a. John paints.
       b. *John plumbs. (compare *plumbing*)

E. 1. a. John was Harry's helper.
       b. John was Harry's benefactor.
    2. a. John helped Harry.
       b. *John benefacted Harry.

F. 1. a. John is a good writer.
       b. John is a good poet.
    2. a. John writes well.
       b. *John poetizes well.

The same grammatical relations seem to hold in the 1.a sentences as in the 1.b sentences. For example, *Harry* in E.1.a bears the same relation to *helper* as it does to *benefactor* in E.1.b. Since *Harry* bears the same relation to *helper* as to *help* in E.2.a, namely, direct object, it therefore bears the relation of direct object to *benefactor* in E.1.b. If we hypothesize the verb *to benefact* and mark it so that it must meet the SD of AGNT-NOM, we can derive E.1.b in the same way as we derive E.1.a and thereby account for these facts. Moreover, we can account for the fact that we understand E.2.b and know that in that nonsentence *Harry* is the object of *benefact* and *John* is the subject of *benefact*.

In F.1, *good* seems to modify *writer* in the same way as it modifies *poet*. But 1.a must be derived from 2.a, which shows that *good* in 1.a must have an adverbial source. This would suggest that *good* in 1.b must also have an adverbial source. We can account for this if we hypothesize the existence of an underlying verb for *poet,* as in F.2.b.

It is difficult to see how any of these facts could be accounted for without hypothesizing underlying verbs for the agent nouns of the 1.b sentences.

6.45 Object Nouns

There exist a number of nouns that are understood in the same way as certain object nouns [see Section 5.12]. For example,

A. What John aimed for was to conquer the world. (6-29)
   1. a. John's aim was to conquer the world.
       b. John's goal was to conquer the world.
   2. a. John aimed to conquer the world.
       b. *John goaled to conquer the world.

B. What Greg intended was to overthrow the government.
   1. a. Greg's intention was to overthrow the government.
       b. Greg's purpose was to overthrow the government.
   2. a. Greg intended to overthrow the government.
       b. *Greg purposed to overthrow the government.

C. What John writes pleases me.
   1. a. I read all of John's writings.
       b. I read all of John's poems.
   2. a. I read all of what John wrote.
       b. *I read all of what John poetized.

D. What John believes shocks me.
   1. a. John's beliefs shock me.
       b. John's ideas shock me.
   2. a. John believes that there is no God.
       b. *John ideates that there is no God.

In the 1.a and 1.b sentences, the same grammatical relations hold. In A, B, and C, the 1.a sentences are systematically related to the 2.a sentences and the grammatical relations in the 1.a sentences must be accounted for in terms of those in the 2.a sentences. But in order to account for the grammatical relations in the 1.b sentences, we must hypothesize underlying verbs (*to goal, to purpose, to poetize*), mark them so that they must meet the SD of OBJ-NOM, and derive the 1.b sentences from structures underlying partially grammatical sentences like those in 2.b. Thus, we could also explain the fact that we understand the 2.b sentences and can make grammatical judgments about them, for instance, that *John* and *that there is no God* bear the same relations, respectively, to *believe* and to *ideate* in D. Again it is difficult to see how these facts could be accounted for without setting up hypothetical underlying verbs.

7 BOOLEAN EXCEPTIONS

So far, we have considered lexical items as having simple conjunctions of SD features and R features. But this assumption is inadequate in certain respects. Consider the case of *aggress*. Note that *aggression* and *aggressor* may both occur, although *aggress* may not. *Aggress*, therefore, must be considered an absolute exception to *both* NOMINALIZATION and AGNT-NOM. That is, *aggress* must meet the SD of NOMINALIZATION to yield *aggression* or it must meet the SD of AGNT-NOM to yield *aggressor*. But if we were to represent *aggress* in the lexicon with a "conjunction" of the features [m SD(NOMINALIZATION)] and [m SD(AGNT-NOM)], we would be asserting that in *each* derivation in which *aggress* could occur it would have to meet the structural descriptions of *both* rules. This is clearly impossible—the environments in which the rules can occur are mutually exclusive. Moreover, it does not accord with the facts, namely, that *aggress* must be transformed *either* into *aggression* or into *aggressor*. That is, it must meet *either* the SD of NOMINALIZATION *or* that of AGNT-NOM. We can account for these facts if we allow the lexicon to contain Boolean functions of SD and R features. The entry for *aggress* could then contain the disjunction of features:

$$[\text{m SD(NOMINALIZATION) (L)}] \lor \qquad (7\text{-}1)$$
$$[\text{m SD(AGNT-NOM) (L)}]$$

which would be conjoined to the other features of *aggress*. Our metarules would convert (7-1) into (7-2):

$$[+\text{SD(NOMINALIZATION) (L)}] \lor \qquad (7\text{-}2)$$
$$[+\text{SD(AGNT-NOM) (L)}]$$

If we maintain the definition of a violation that we have already established [see Sections 1.52 and E.4], the representation of *aggress* in (7-2) will yield violations whenever the SDs of *neither* of the rules have been met. If either SD has been met, there will be no violation. [See Remark 7-1.]

Note that in order to handle Boolean exceptions such as this one we *need* Postal's lexical substitution rule and a definition of a violation like the one given in Section 1.51. Given a condition on a lexical item such as (7-2), there is in general only one way of telling whether a lexical item which has been substituted into a given deep structure will meet this condition—namely, by applying the transformational rules and carrying out all possible derivations. That is, Boolean exceptions state conditions which must be met in the course of an *entire* transformational derivation, rather than in the application of a single rule. The *only* way of handling exceptions of this sort, therefore, is to keep track of what happens in the course of a derivation and then check to see whether the conditions on individual lexical items have been violated.

Since it is in general impossible to tell on the basis of deep structure alone whether or not the choice of a given lexical item will lead to a violation, and since we must carry out a transformational derivation to discover this, there will, of necessity, be cases in which deviant sentences must be directly generated and marked as to the degree and nature of their deviance. Thus, we find that our choice of the Postal lexical substitution rule is well-motivated on factual as well as esthetic grounds.

Let us look at some other cases of Boolean exceptions. The following examples are similar to the *aggressor-aggression* pair: *criminal-crime, adulterer-adultery, aviator-aviation, felon-felony,* and so on. A somewhat different example is the verb *to transform.* Compare *transform* and *change* in the following examples:

1. a. Bill changed John into a werewolf.   (7-3)
   b. Bill transformed John into a werewolf.
2. a. Bill's changing of John into a werewolf
   b. Bill's transformation of John into a werewolf
3. a. John's change into a werewolf
   b. John's transformation into a werewolf
4. a. John changed into a werewolf.
   b. *John transformed into a werewolf.

Transform and *change* are synonymous in these examples.

Each a example is understood in the same way as its corresponding b example—and the same grammatical relations and co-occurrence restrictions hold in each pair. This is true even in 4. Although 4.b occurs only as a deviant sentence, it is understood in the same way as 4.a, which is fully grammatical. In both 1 and 2, *change* and *transform* have both undergone the CAUSATIVE transformation. In 3 and 4, neither of them has undergone that rule. The fact that 4.b cannot occur reflects the fact that *transform* has the following restriction associated with it in the lexicon: *transform* must either meet the SD of CAUSATIVE or it must meet the SD of NOMINALIZATION; a violation results if *transform* occurs in a sentence without having undergone one of these two rules. We would represent this restriction in the lexicon with the following disjunction of marked SD features:

[m SD(CAUSATIVE)] ∨   (7-4)
[m SD(NOMINALIZATION)]

Thus, *transform* is a Boolean exception in much the same way as *aggress* is.

Another such example is the pair *sharp* and *sharpen*. Consider the following:

1. a. The metal is hard.   (7-5)
   b. The knife is sharp.
2. a. The metal hardened.
   b. *The knife sharpened.
3. a. John hardened the metal.
   b. John sharpened the knife.

Sentences 2 are derived from sentences 1 by the INCHOATIVE transformation. The further application of the CAUSATIVE transformation yields the 3 sentences. [See Sections 5.15 and 5.16.] Although 3.a and 3.b are derived in the same way, 2.b, the intermediate step in the derivation of 3.b, is somewhat deviant, while 2.a is fully grammatical. Still, we understand 2.b and we know that it is related to 1.b and 3.b in the same way as 2.a is related to 1.a and 3.a. The fact that 2.b does not occur seems to indicate that *sharp* is represented in the lexicon with the following restriction: if *sharp* undergoes the INCHOATIVE transformation, it must also meet the SD of the CAUSATIVE transformation (and, of course, undergo the CAUSATIVE rule). We would represent this restriction in the following way:

[m SD(INCHOATIVE)] ⊃ [m SD(CAUSATIVE)]   (7-6)

Our metarules will change this into:

[+SD(INCHOATIVE)] ⊃ [+SD(CAUSATIVE)]   (7-7)

which is simply a statement of the restriction. [See Section 8.3.]

These examples indicate that Boolean exceptions are by no means rare and that one does not have to search far to find a wide variety of them.

8 OPTIONALITY

8.1 OPTIONAL EXCEPTIONS TO OBLIGATORY RULES

There exist cases in which an item may optionally undergo a rule that is normally obligatory. Consider P. S. Rosenbaum's pronoun-deletion transformation, which we will refer to as IT-DEL [see Rosenbaum, 1967, Chapters 1 and 4]. It is normally the case that an unspecified pronoun (*it*) is deleted when it immediately precedes an embedded sentence. Consider the following:

1. a. It is believed by Bill that John loves Mary.   (8-1)
   b. *Bill believes it that John loves Mary.
   c. Bill believes that John loves Mary.
2. a. It is known by everyone that John loves Mary.
   b. *Everyone knows it that John loves Mary.
   c. Everyone knows that John loves Mary.

In the a sentences, the passive has been applied and the embedded sentence *that John loves Mary* has been shifted to the end *prior* to the application of IT-DEL. Since the environment for IT-DEL is not met, that is, since *it* does not immediately precede an embedded sentence, the *it* does not drop. In the b and c sentences the passive has not applied, and *it* occurs before an embedded sentence. If *it* does not drop, we get a violation, as in the b examples. If *it* does drop, the result is the fully grammatical c sentences.

The verb *hate*, however, is exceptional in that the *it* may or may not be deleted.

   a. I hate it for John to do that.   (8-2)
   b. I hate for John to do that.

Although IT-DEL is an obligatory rule, *hate* may optionally undergo that rule.

Optional exceptions like *hate* can be handled within the framework that we have already set up. The basic fact about optional exceptions to some rule is that the application or nonapplication of that rule can never produce a violation in these cases. In terms of plus- and minus-valued rule features, this means that neither a plus- nor a minus-valued grammatical rule feature can produce a contradiction in conjunction with the lexical representation of the exceptional item. This will be true if the lexical item contains the plus-minus representation:

$$\left[[+R(IT\text{-}DEL)] \lor [-R(IT\text{-}DEL)] \right] \qquad (8\text{-}3)$$

This simply says that IT-DEL may freely apply or not apply without yielding a violation. Note that (8-3) is equivalent to (8-4).

$$\left[[-R(IT\text{-}DEL)] \supset [-R(IT\text{-}DEL)] \right] \qquad (8\text{-}4)$$

And our metarules will produce (8-4) from (8-5).

$$\left[[m\ R(IT\text{-}DEL)] \supset [m\ R(IT\text{-}DEL)] \right] \qquad (8\text{-}5)$$

Thus, we can account for the facts of (8-2) if our lexical representation of *hate* contains (8-5). Other optional exceptions to obligatory rules can be handled in the same way.

8.2 EXCEPTIONS TO OPTIONAL RULES

In our discussion of exceptions to obligatory rules, we found it necessary to postulate two types of binary exception features: SD features and R features. These features, combined in Boolean functions, provided a well-defined and fairly narrow specification of the range of possible exceptions to syntactic transformations—compared to the infinite range of possibilities permitted by arbitrary subcategorization. For each major rule, i, our binary exception features defined four basic possibilities:

1. u SD(i) (8-6)
    and u R(i):   The unmarked or "normal" case: The item may or may not meet the structural description of i, but if it does, it *must* undergo i.

2. u SD(i)
and m R(i):   Simple exception:
               The item may meet the struc-
               tural description of i, but may
               not undergo i.

3. m SD(i)
and u R(i):   Positive absolute exception:
               The item must meet the struc-
               tural description of i and, there-
               fore, must undergo i.

4. m SD(i)
and m R(i):   Negative absolute exception:
               The item must not meet the struc-
               tural description of i.

However, in the case of optional rules there seem to be not four, but five, logical possibilities:

1. The "normal" case for optional rules: (8-7)
   The item may or may not meet the structural
   description, and if it does not, it may or may not
   undergo the rule. No violation is possible.
2. Obligatory exception:
   Same as 1 in (8-6): the item may or may not
   meet the structural description of Rule i, but if
   does it *must* undergo i.
3. Negative exception:
   Same as 2 in (8-6): the item may meet the structural description of i, but may not undergo i.
4. Positive absolute exception:
   Same as 3 in (8-6).
5. Negative absolute exception:
   Same as 4 in (8-6).

Possibility 1 in (8-7): An example is any "normal" item to which an optional rule can apply. For instance, *look up* is normal with respect to the particle shift rule. Thus, we can get either *John looked up the information* or *John looked the information up*. Or consider *tall* with respect to WH-DEL: we can get either *the boy who is tall* or *the tall boy* (with the subsequent obligatory application of ADJ-SHIFT).

Possibility 2 in (8-7): An example is any verb that takes a particle and must undergo the particle shift rule if the SD of that rule is met: *bring to* and *put on* (meaning "to tease, joke with, or kid"). We get *The doctor brought the patient to* but not **The doctor* *brought to the patient.* Similarly, we get *John was putting Bill on* but not **John was putting on Bill.*

Possibility 3 in (8-7) : There seem to be no examples of this phenomenon. In Section 5.4, we claimed, for the sake of exposition of a different point, that adjectives like *content* were examples of this phenomenon, that is, that such adjectives could not undergo WH-DEL. We considered the examples *the boy who is content* but not **the boy content* or **the content boy.* However, the fact that we can get *the boy content with his lot* shows that this analysis is wrong. [For discussion, see Remark 8-1.] If we could not get *the boy content with his lot,* then we might have a case for the existence of this phenomenon.

Possibility 4 in (8-7) : Some examples are *gala, late* (meaning "deceased") and *poor* (meaning "unfortunate"). These must meet the SD of WH-DEL and undergo that rule. They may never occur in simple sentences or in relative clauses, but only in prenominal position. Thus, if *poor* has the meaning "unfortunate" we get only *the poor man,* not **the man who is poor* or **the man is poor.* Similarly we get *a gala event,* but not **an event which was gala* or **the event is gala.*

Possibility 5 in (8-7) : We have found no examples of this phenomenon. It would be easy to see what such an example might be like, were one to exist. Imagine an adjective *zilch,* which could occur only in simple sentences, but never in relative clauses or as a noun modifier, either prenominal or postnominal. *Zilch* could then be described as unable to meet the structural description of WH-DEL, and would be a negative absolute exception to an optional rule.

Since our two binary exception features define only four basic cases, they are not sufficient to define the five logically possible cases of (8-7). In order to incorporate a treatment of optional rules into the descriptive framework we have set up so far, we will make use of the fact that only three of the five possibilities have actually been found, and we will assume that only these three are possible. Should one of the two cases we have excluded ever turn up, then the metarules that we will give below will have to be revised. Should both of these cases turn up, our entire descriptive framework (two types of exception features) would prove to be inadequate and would have to be broadened.

Of possibilities 1, 2, and 4 described in (8-7), 1 is the "normal" case, while 2 and 4 are less so. We can account for this by assigning values of exception features to these cases in the following way:

a. u SD(i) and u R(i) : normal case, 1 in (8-7)   (8-8)
b. u SD(i) and m R(i) : obligatory exception, 2 in (8-7)

    c. m SD(i) and u R(i) : positive absolute exception,
       4 in (8-7)
    d. m SD(1) and m R(i) : does not exist

Note that obligatory cases work in optional rules just as normal cases work in obligatory rules [compare 2 in (8-7) and 1 in (8-6)]. And positive absolute exceptions work the same way in both obligatory and optional rules [compare 4 in (8-7) and 3 in (8-6)]. We will account for this in the following way. We will set up metarules that will operate on exception features that correspond to optional rules. These metarules will apply prior to the application of Metarules 1 through 5. They will map normal cases for optional rules into the appropriate pluses and minuses, and they will map the other optional rule cases into the corresponding obligatory rule cases. Metarules 1 through 5 will then operate on the output of these metarules.

    Metarules for optional rule cases: For optional rules i:

$$(8\text{-}9)$$

A. $[\text{u R(i) (L)}] \rightarrow [\alpha \text{ R(i) (L)}] \,/\, \begin{bmatrix} \text{u SD(i) (L)} \\ \alpha \text{ R(i) (G)} \end{bmatrix}$

B. $[\text{m R(i) (L)}] \rightarrow [\text{u R(i) (L)}]$

As with minor rules [see Section 5.2], we can consider the optional rules to be given in a list, in which each member is to be assigned the same integer by our evaluation procedure. Our theory would include a mechanical procedure which takes the list of optional rules as input and produces specific metarules of the form of (8-9). For instance, if 73 were on the list of optional rules, there would be a set of metarules of the form:

$$(8\text{-}10)$$

A. $[\text{u R(73) (L)}] \rightarrow [\alpha \text{ R(73) (L)}] \,/\, \begin{bmatrix} \text{u SD(73) (L)} \\ \alpha \text{ R(73) (G)} \end{bmatrix}$

B. $[\text{m R(73) (L)}] \rightarrow [\text{u R(73) (L)}]$

These metarules operate in the following manner. A captures the fact that in normal cases, optional rules can never yield a violation. In our system, we have defined a violation as a contradiction between grammatical and lexical R features. Metarule A guarantees that for normal optional rule cases such a contradiction can never occur. What A does is to assimilate the value of the lexical R feature to that of the grammatical R feature, that is, it makes sure that their values will always be the same. Thus, if the grammatical member of the complex symbol in question contains

$$\left[\begin{array}{lll} & u\ SD\,(73)\ (L) \\ -R\,(73)\ (G) & , & u\ R\,(73)\ (L) \end{array} \right] \qquad (8\text{-}11)$$

that is, if rule 73 has not applied, A will map (8-11) into (8-12).

$$\left[\begin{array}{lll} & u\ SD\,(73)\ (L) \\ -R\,(73)\ (G) & , & -R\,(73)\ (L) \end{array} \right] \qquad (8\text{-}12)$$

If on the other hand, Rule 73 *has* applied, the complex symbol will contain:

$$\left[\begin{array}{lll} & u\ SD\,(73)\ (L) \\ +R\,(73)\ (G) & , & +R\,(73)\ (L) \end{array} \right] \qquad (8\text{-}13)$$

Metarule B maps obligatory exceptions to optional rules like b in (8-8) into normal cases for obligatory rules like 1 in (8-6). For example, B will map:

$$\begin{array}{l} u\ SD\,(73)\ (L) \\ m\ R\,(73)\ (L) \end{array} \qquad (8\text{-}14)$$

into:

$$\begin{array}{l} u\ SD\,(73)\ (L) \\ u\ R\,(73)\ (L) \end{array} \qquad (8\text{-}15)$$

Note that B will also map the representation:

$$\begin{array}{l} m\ SD\,(73)\ (L) \\ m\ R\,(73)\ (L) \end{array} \qquad (8\text{-}16)$$

into the positive absolute exception case:

$$\begin{array}{l} m\ SD\,(73)\ (L) \\ u\ R\,(73)\ (L) \end{array} \qquad (8\text{-}17)$$

Since the lexical representation of the form:

$$\begin{array}{l} m\ SD\,(73)\ (L) \\ u\ SD\,(73)\ (L) \end{array} \qquad (8\text{-}18)$$

is unchanged by Metarules A and B, we have two sources of positive absolute exceptions: those which start out in the lexicon in the form (8-18) and those which start out in the lexicon as (8-16). That is, these different lexical representations will be indistinguishable as to the way they will operate in any grammar. Since our evaluation measure will always prefer lexicons with the fewest m's, representations of the form (8-16) will never occur in any grammar defined by our theory and to which our evaluation measure has been applied. This effectively rules out representations of the form (8-16) for optional rules.

Just as in the case of our formalism for minor rules, metarules of the form of (8-9) have no direct linguistic interpretation and make sense only in the context of the other theoretical apparatus that we have set up.

8.3 CANONICAL FORM OF IRREGULARITY REPRESENTATIONS

We must impose more structure on lexical items than simply allowing them to contain Boolean functions of marked and unmarked features. We will consider the canonical form of that part of a lexical item that indicates irregularities to consist of a conjunction of four parts:

1. a. marked SD part
   b. marked R part $\Big\}$ marked part (unpredictable part)

2. a. unmarked SD part
   b. unmarked R part $\Big\}$ unmarked part (predictable part)

The marked SD part will be a Boolean function of "marked" SD features. The marked R part will be a conjunction of:

(a) marked R features
(b) implications of the form: [m R(X)] $\supset$ [m R(X)], where R(X) is not in (a).

Optional exceptions to obligatory rules take the b form.
   The unmarked SD part will consist of a conjunction of unmarked SD features, for *all* of the SD features defined by the grammar—*including* those mentioned in the marked SD part. The unmarked R part will consist of a conjunction of unmarked R features, for all R features defined by the grammar—*except* those mentioned in the marked R part.

We will refer to these marked and unmarked parts together as the "irregularity representation" of the lexical item (IR). Note that given the marked part of an IR, the unmarked part is entirely predictable. Since this is the case, we need not mention the unmarked part of the IR in the lexicon, but can have it filled in by a mechanical procedure after each lexical item has been substituted into a deep structure defined by the grammar.

Consider the following example. Assume (for the sake of simplicity) that we have a grammar with seven rules. Assume that the lexicon contains the following item:

glok and ([m SD(2)] ⊃ [m SD(4)]) and ([m R(5)]⊃
[m R(5)] and [m R(6)]
Marked SD part: [m SD(2)] ⊃ [m SD(4)]
Marked R part: ([m R(5)] ⊃ [m R(5)]) and [m R(6)]

We could now predict that *glok* would have the following unmarked parts:

Unmarked SD part: [u SD(1)] and [u SD(2)] and [u SD(3)]
and [u SD(4)] and [u SD(5)] and [u SD(6)] and [u SD(7)]
Unmarked R part: [u R(1)] and [u R(2)] and [u R(3)] and
[u R(4)] and [u R(7)]

In the canonical representation that we have just given, SD features and R features play rather different roles. R features represent only simple exceptions—cases where an item may not undergo a major rule or may undergo a minor rule. The implications of the form ([m R(X)] ⊃ [m R(X)]) represent only optional exceptions to obligatory rules. All other restrictions are stated in terms of SD features. The most interesting of these restrictions are those that involve constraints between rules: lexical items that must undergo one rule if they have undergone another [see (7-6)]. First we will show that such constraints can be given in terms of SD features alone, and then we will show why they cannot be stated in terms of R features.

Recall that our metarules are:

1. [m R(i) (L)] → [−R(i) (L)]

2. [m SD(i) (L)] → [−SD(i) (L)] / $\boxed{-R(i) \quad (L)}$

3. [u SD(i) (L)] → [α SD(i) (L)] / $\boxed{α\,SD(i) \quad (G)}$

4. [m SD(i) (L)] → [+SD(i) (L)]

5. [u R(i) (L)] → [α R(i) (L)] / $\boxed{α\,SD(i) \quad (L)}$

Let us assume, for simplicity, that our grammar has only two rules. Consider the following lexical item:

gurk and ([m SD(1)] ⊃ [m SD (2)])

The restriction on *gurk* states that if Rule 1 applies, then Rule 2 must also apply. It is not obvious that the restriction does state this. Since the restriction is given in terms of SD features, it appears to say something like "if the SD of 1 is met, then the SD of 2 must be met, though Rules 1 and 2 may or may not apply." That is, the restriction seems to embody a statement about structural descriptions being met, not about rule application. But this is not the case. Because Metarule 5 assimilates unmarked R features to their corresponding SD features, the restriction on *gurk* turns out to be a restriction on the application of the corresponding rules.

To show this we will consider three cases:

Case 1: Neither structural description is met and neither Rule 1 nor Rule 2 applies. Result: no violation.
Case 2: Rule 1 applies, but Rule 2 does not. Result: violation.
Case 3: Both Rule 1 and Rule 2 apply. Result: no violation.

Case 1. Before any *m*'s and *u*'s have been converted to minuses and pluses, and before the unmarked part has been predicted, we would have:

$$
\begin{bmatrix}
-\text{SD}(1)\ (\text{G}) & \\
-\text{R}(1)\ (\text{G}) & ([\text{m SD}(1)\ (\text{L})] \supset [\text{m SD}(2)\ (\text{L})]) \\
-\text{SD}(2)\ (\text{G}) & \\
-\text{R}(2)\ (\text{G}) & ,\quad gurk
\end{bmatrix}
$$

After predicting the unmarked part of the IR of *gurk:*

$$
\begin{bmatrix}
-\text{SD}(1)\ (\text{G}) & ([\text{m SD}(1)\ (\text{L})] \supset [\text{m SD}(2)\ (\text{L})]) \\
-\text{R}(1)\ (\text{G}) & \text{u SD}(1)\ (\text{L}) \\
-\text{SD}(2)\ (\text{G}) & \text{u SD}(2)\ (\text{L}) \\
-\text{R}(2)\ (\text{G}) & \text{u R}(1)\ (\text{L}) \\
& \text{u R}(2)\ (\text{L}) \\
& ,\quad gurk
\end{bmatrix}
$$

Metarules 1 and 2 are irrelevant and do not operate. Metarule 3 does operate:

$$
\begin{bmatrix}
-\text{SD}(1)\ (\text{G}) & ([\text{m SD}(1)\ (\text{L})] \supset [\text{m SD}(2)\ (\text{L})]) \\
-\text{R}(1)\ (\text{G}) & -\text{SD}(1)\ (\text{L}) \\
-\text{SD}(2)\ (\text{G}) & -\text{SD}(2)\ (\text{L}) \\
-\text{R}(2)\ (\text{G}) & \text{u R}(1)\ (\text{L}) \\
& \text{u R}(2)\ (\text{L}) \\
& ,\quad gurk
\end{bmatrix}
$$

After Metarule 4 operates, we have:

$$
\begin{bmatrix}
\begin{array}{ll}
\text{—SD(1) (G)} & \text{([+SD(1) (L)]} \supset \text{[+SD(2) (L)])} \\
\text{—R(1) (G)} & \text{—SD(1) (L)} \\
\text{—SD(2) (G)} & \text{—SD(2) (L)} \\
\text{—R(2) (G)} & \text{u R(1) (L)} \\
& \text{u R(2) (L)} \\
\quad , \ \textit{gurk}
\end{array}
\end{bmatrix}
$$

We must now make our definition of Metarule 5 somewhat more precise. As things now stand, it is not clear whether the unmarked rule features should turn out plus or minus by Metarule 5. That is, it is not clear whether the lexical SD feature referred to in the environment of Metarule 5 is the minus-valued SD feature that originated in the unmarked SD part or the plus-valued SD feature that is in the Boolean function of the marked SD part. We will assume that the former is always the case. That is, the lexical SD feature referred to in the environment of Metarule 5 will always be interpreted as the one that was introduced in the unmarked SD part.

Now Metarule 5 will yield:

$$
\begin{bmatrix}
\begin{array}{ll}
\text{—SD(1) (G)} & \text{([+SD(1) (L)]} \supset \text{[+SD(2) (L)])} \\
\text{—R(1) (G)} & \text{—SD(1) (L)} \\
\text{—SD(2) (G)} & \text{—SD(2) (L)} \\
\text{—R(2) (G)} & \text{—R(1) (L)} \\
& \text{—R(2) (L)} \\
\quad , \ \textit{gurk}
\end{array}
\end{bmatrix}
$$

The result is that there is no violation.

There still remains the question of how our metarules are to distinguish a lexical SD feature which originated in the unmarked SD part from one which originated in the marked SD part. One could solve the problem either by keeping the parts distinct or by changing Metarule 5 to read:

$$5': \ [\text{u R(i) (L)}] \rightarrow [\alpha \text{ R(i) (L)}] \ / \ \boxed{\underline{\alpha \text{ SD(i) (G)}}}$$

That is, we could assimilate the unmarked R features to their corresponding *grammatical* SD features. Note that we could still not eliminate the unmarked SD part, since its presence is necessary if we are to state rules such as (VII) in Remark 8-1.

We will assume the latter solution. We will adopt Metarule 5′ above instead of Metarule 5. Let us now consider Cases 2 and 3.

Case 2. Before any m's and u's have been converted to minuses and pluses, and before the unmarked part has been predicted, we would have:

$$
\begin{bmatrix}
+\text{SD}(1) \quad (\text{G}) & ([\text{m SD}(i)\ (\text{L})] \supset [\text{m SD}(2)\ (\text{L})]) \\
+\text{R}(1) \quad (\text{G}) \\
-\text{SD}(2) \quad (\text{G}) \\
-\text{R}(2) \quad (\text{G}) \quad , \quad gurk
\end{bmatrix}
$$

After predicting the unmarked part we have:

$$
\begin{bmatrix}
+\text{SD}(1) \quad (\text{G}) & ([\text{m SD}(i)\ (\text{L})] \supset [\text{m SD}(2)\ (\text{L})]) \\
+\text{R}(1) \quad (\text{G}) & \text{u SD}(1)\ (\text{L}) \\
-\text{SD}(2) \quad (\text{G}) & \text{u SD}(2)\ (\text{L}) \\
-\text{R}(2) \quad (\text{G}) & \text{u R}(1)\ (\text{L}) \\
& \text{u R}(2)\ (\text{L}) \\
& , \quad gurk
\end{bmatrix}
$$

Metarules 1 and 2 are irrelevant and do not operate. Metarules 3 and 4 yield:

$$
\begin{bmatrix}
+\text{SD}(1) \quad (\text{G}) & ([+\text{SD}(1)\ (\text{L})] \supset [+\text{SD}(2)\ (\text{L})]) \\
+\text{R}(1) \quad (\text{G}) & +\text{SD}(1)\ (\text{L}) \\
-\text{SD}(2) \quad (\text{G}) & -\text{SD}(2)\ (\text{L}) \\
-\text{R}(2) \quad (\text{G}) & \text{u R}(1)\ (\text{L}) \\
& \text{u R}(2)\ (\text{L}) \\
& , \quad gurk
\end{bmatrix}
$$

Our new Metarule 5′ will now give us:

$$
\begin{bmatrix}
+\text{SD}(1) \quad (\text{G}) & ([+\text{SD}(1)\ (\text{L})] \supset [+\text{SD}(2)\ (\text{L})]) \\
+\text{R}(1) \quad (\text{G}) & +\text{SD}(1)\ (\text{L}) \\
-\text{SD}(2) \quad (\text{G}) & -\text{SD}(2)\ (\text{L}) \\
-\text{R}(2) \quad (\text{G}) & +\text{R}(1)\ (\text{L}) \\
& -\text{R}(2)\ (\text{L}) \\
& , \quad gurk
\end{bmatrix}
$$

This yields a violation.

Case 3. Before any m's and u's have been converted to minuses and pluses, and before the unmarked R part has been predicted we would have:

$$
\begin{bmatrix}
\begin{array}{ll}
+\text{SD}(1) \ (\text{G}) & [\text{m SD}(1) \ (\text{L})] \supset [\text{m SD}(2) \ (\text{L})] \\
+\text{R}(1) \ (\text{G}) & \\
+\text{SD}(2) \ (\text{G}) & \\
+\text{R}(2) \ (\text{G}) & , \ gurk
\end{array}
\end{bmatrix}
$$

After the unmarked R part has been predicted, we would have:

$$
\begin{bmatrix}
\begin{array}{ll}
+\text{SD}(1) \ (\text{G}) & [\text{m SD}(1) \ (\text{L})] \supset [\text{m SD}(2) \ (\text{L})] \\
+\text{R}(1) \ (\text{G}) & \text{u SD}(1) \ (\text{L}) \\
+\text{SD}(2) \ (\text{G}) & \text{u SD}(2) \ (\text{L}) \\
+\text{R}(2) \ (\text{G}) & \text{u R}(1) \ (\text{L}) \\
& \text{u R}(2) \ (\text{L}) \\
& , \ gurk
\end{array}
\end{bmatrix}
$$

Metarules 3 and 4 yield:

$$
\begin{bmatrix}
\begin{array}{ll}
+\text{SD}(1) \ (\text{G}) & ([+\text{SD}(1) \ (\text{L})] \supset [+\text{SD}(2) \ (\text{L})]) \\
+\text{R}(1) \ (\text{G}) & +\text{SD}(1) \ (\text{L}) \\
+\text{SD}(2) \ (\text{G}) & +\text{SD}(2) \ (\text{L}) \\
+\text{R}(2) \ (\text{G}) & \text{u R}(1) \ (\text{L}) \\
& \text{u R}(2) \ (\text{L}) \\
& , \ gurk
\end{array}
\end{bmatrix}
$$

Metarule 5′ yields:

$$
\begin{bmatrix}
\begin{array}{ll}
+\text{SD}(1) \ (\text{G}) & [+\text{SD}(1) \ (\text{L})] \supset [+\text{SD}(2) \ (\text{L})] \\
+\text{R}(1) \ (\text{G}) & +\text{SD}(1) \ (\text{L}) \\
+\text{SD}(2) \ (\text{G}) & +\text{SD}(2) \ (\text{L}) \\
+\text{R}(2) \ (\text{G}) & +\text{R}(1) \ (\text{L}) \\
& +\text{R}(2) \ (\text{L}) \\
& , \ gurk
\end{array}
\end{bmatrix}
$$

The result is no violation.

So far we have shown that a restriction of the form ([m SD(1)] $\supset$ [m SD(2)]) is a restriction on rules that states that if Rule 1 applies, Rule 2 must also apply. We have not yet shown that this is not a statement about structural descriptions. To show this we would have to show that if both structural descriptions were met, we would still get a violation unless both rules also applied. This is true since Metarule 5′ requires a rule to apply if its SD has been met. For example, suppose both structural descriptions were met, but neither rule had applied. After the prediction of the unmarked R part of *gurk* and the application of Metarule 4, we would have:

$$
\begin{bmatrix}
\begin{array}{ll}
+\text{SD}(1)\ (\text{G}) & ([+\text{SD}(1)\ (\text{L})] \supset [+\text{SD}(2)\ (\text{L})]) \\
-\text{R}(1)\ (\text{G}) & +\text{SD}(1)\ (\text{L}) \\
+\text{SD}(2)\ (\text{G}) & +\text{SD}(2)\ (\text{L}) \\
-\text{R}(2)\ (\text{G}) & u\ \text{R}(1)\ (\text{L}) \\
 & u\ \text{R}(2)\ (\text{L}) \\
 & ,\ gurk
\end{array}
\end{bmatrix}
$$

Metarule 5′ yields:

$$
\begin{bmatrix}
\begin{array}{ll}
+\text{SD}(1)\ (\text{G}) & [+\text{SD}(1)\ (\text{L})] \supset [+\text{SD}(2)\ (\text{L})] \\
-\text{R}(1)\ (\text{G}) & +\text{SD}(1)\ (\text{L}) \\
+\text{SD}(2)\ (\text{G}) & +\text{SD}(2)\ (\text{L}) \\
-\text{R}(2)\ (\text{G}) & +\text{R}(1)\ (\text{L}) \\
 & +\text{R}(2)\ (\text{L}) \\
 & ,\ gurk
\end{array}
\end{bmatrix}
$$

The result is a violation.

Our revised metarules are:

1. $[\text{m R}(i)\ (\text{L})] \rightarrow [-\text{R}(i)\ (\text{L})]$

2. $[\text{m SD}(i)\ (\text{L})] \rightarrow [-\text{SD}(i)\ (\text{L})]\ /\ \boxed{-\text{R}(i)\ (\text{L})}$

3. $[\text{u SD}(i)\ (\text{L})] \rightarrow [\alpha\ \text{SD}(i)\ (\text{L})]\ /\ \boxed{\alpha\ \text{SD}(i)\ (\text{G})}$

4. $[\text{m SD}(i)\ (\text{L})] \rightarrow [+\text{SD}(i)\ (\text{L})]$

5′. $[\text{u R}(i)\ (\text{L})] \rightarrow [\alpha\ \text{R}(i)\ (\text{L})]\ /\ \boxed{\alpha\ \text{SD}(i)\ (\text{G})}$

9 LEXICAL REPRESENTATION

9.1 THE STRUCTURE OF LEXICAL ITEMS

When a word has a number of different senses, it is usually the case that these senses are differentiated by having different grammatical properties. Take, for example, the word *hard*.

a. The rock is hard.   (9-1)
b. The work is hard.

In Sentence a *hard* means "solid" and in b *hard* means "difficult." Note that b is a reduced form of

The work is hard for someone.   (9-2)

Hard is one of those adjectives that undergoes FLIP [see Section A.6]. Thus, the underlying subject of (9-2) is *someone* while the underlying object is *the work*. Since FLIP is a minor rule, sense b of *hard* must be marked for undergoing that rule. (Sense a is unmarked of course since it could never undergo FLIP.) Thus, sense b of *hard* must contain the feature [m R(FLIP)].

Note that *hard* in sense b cannot be nominalized, while it can be in sense a.

1. a. The rock is hard.   (9-3)
    b. The hardness of the rock
2. a. The work is hard.
    b. *The hardness of the work
3. a. The work is difficult.
    b. The difficulty of the work

Thus, *hard* in sense b is an exception to the nominalization transformation (which is major), while *hard* in sense a is not.

Hard in sense a has certain exceptional properties that sense b does not have. Consider the following:

1. a. The metal is hard. (9-4)
   b. The metal hardened.
   c. John hardened the metal.
2. a. The problem is hard.
   b. *The problem hardened.
   c. *John hardened the problem.

Hard in sense a may undergo both the INCHOATIVE and the CAUSATIVE, while sense b may undergo neither. Since both of those rules are minor, sense a must be marked for being able to undergo them.

The dictionary entry for *hard* would then have to be specified (incompletely, of course) by the following Boolean function:

$$hard \text{ and } \lceil [\langle \text{difficult} \rangle \text{ and } m \text{ R(FLIP) and} \qquad (9\text{-}5)$$

$$m \text{ R(NOMINALIZATION)}] \text{ or } [\langle \text{solid} \rangle \text{ and}$$

$$m \text{ R(INCHOATIVE) and } m \text{ R(CAUSATIVE)}] \rceil$$

To take a somewhat more complicated example, consider the word *operate* in a few of its senses.

Sense 1: To cause to function by direct personal effort.
Sense 2: To relate one set of mathematical entities to another by a definite rule.
Sense 3: To perform surgery.
Sense 4: To run a telephone switchboard.
Sense 5: To get one's way by shrewdly and skillfully evading or circumventing restrictions, controls, or difficulty.

In each of these senses *operate* has somewhat different grammatical restrictions. We will consider only the restrictions with respect to AGNT-NOM and NOMINALIZATION (both of which are major rules).

(The following usages occur in my own idiolect. Others may have different restrictions on the usage of *operate*. We will discuss such idiolectal variation briefly in Section 9.2.)

Sense 1: a. John operates a lathe. (9-6)
   b. John is the operator of a lathe.

Sense 2:
c. John received an award for his skillful operation of the lathe.
a. When d/dx operates on x^2, the result is 2x.
b. d/dx is an operator.
c. The operation of d/dx on x^2 yields 2x.

Sense 3:
a. Doctor Caligari operated on Mrs. Hicks.
b. *Doctor Caligari is a good operator.
c. Doctor Caligari received an award for his skillful operation on Mrs. Hicks.

Sense 4:
a. *Sylvia operates at the telephone company.
b. Sylvia is an operator at the telephone company.
c. *Sylvia received an award for her excellent operation.

Sense 5:
a. You should see Tom operate!
b. Tom is an operator.
c. *I was dismayed by Tom's operation.

We could represent this information in a lexical item in the following way:

(9-7)

operate and [⟨sense 1⟩ or ⟨sense 2⟩] or [⟨sense 3⟩ and m R(AGNT)] or [⟨sense 4⟩ and m SD(AGNT)] or [⟨sense 5⟩ and m R(NOM)]

Almost all verbs have restrictions of this sort, and most verbs have restrictions that are considerably more complicated.

9.2 IDIOLECTAL VARIATIONS IN THE LEXICON

Vocabulary is an extremely fluid area of language. It varies greatly from person to person, both in size and in content, and is capable of being changed extensively. In this section we will look at one of the number of ways in which one person's vocabulary may differ from another's.

In Section 6.42, we remarked that the verb to aggress does not exist, although two of its derived forms, aggression and aggressor, do. This is true for most speakers of English. However, there are English speakers for whom aggress is a perfectly normal verb. Webster's Third New International Dictionary quotes Adlai Stevenson and the Saturday Review as using the verb. For a minority of English speakers, the verb certainly does exist. We would like to raise the question of how idiolectal variations of this sort can be represented in a theory of language. More precisely, we will consider two (hypothetical) speakers of English whose vocabularies differ only in that Speaker 1's vocabulary contains the verb *to aggress*, whereas Speaker 2's does not. We will assume that both vocabularies contain *aggressor* and *aggression*.

As we pointed out in Section 6.43 and Chapter 7, we must assume the lexicon of Speaker 2 contains an entry for *aggress*, in order to account for Speaker 2's knowledge of the relationship between *aggressor* and *aggression* and for his ability to understand deviant sentences in which the verb *to aggress* appears. However, since Speaker 2 will consider every sentence containing *aggress* as deviant, the entry for *aggress* in his lexicon must be considered as containing the Boolean function of exception features given in (7-1). Since *aggress* is a normal verb for Speaker 1, its representation in Speaker 1's lexicon will not contain the exception features of (7-1). In every other way, the representations for *aggress* will be identical in the lexicons of Speaker 1 and Speaker 2. Thus, the lexicons of the two speakers will differ only in that one contains an irregularity restriction that the other does not contain. Note that although there is a sense in which Speaker 1 knows a word that Speaker 2 does not know (namely, *aggress*), the lexicon of Speaker 2 is decidedly more complex than that of Speaker 1. For Speaker 1, *aggress* is a completely regular verb, whereas for Speaker 2, *aggress* is quite irregular.

One of the ways in which the lexicons of two speakers may differ is that one may contain irregularities that the other does not contain. In the case of *aggress* the difference between Speaker 1 and Speaker 2 was quite noticeable—so noticeable that one speaker appeared to know a word that another speaker did not know. However, differences of this sort may be much more subtle. In Section 8.1 we pointed out that *hate* is an optional exception to *it*-deletion. This is true in my own idiolect and in the idiolects of many people I know. But it is by no means true for most speakers of English. There are many people for whom *I hate it for John to go* is a deviant sentence, while *I hate for John to go* is not deviant for them. Such people do not have the Boolean function of exception features given in (8-5) associated with the item *hate* in their lexicons. In this respect, my lexicon is somewhat more complex than theirs.

The fact that some people use *hate* in a slightly different way than other people do—some people require *it*-deletion, others do not—should not make a linguist despair that his facts are unclear. In this case, the facts are quite clear—and they must be accounted for. Two people may have the same rules of grammar, but if they have different irregularities in their lexicons, they will not consider the same set of sentences as being grammatical. It is not unusual for two people to have different irregularities in their lexicons. In fact, it would be unusual for two people to have exactly the same irregularities in their lexicons—that is, it would be unusual for two people to use all of the words they both know in exactly the same way.

9.3 LEXICAL BASE AND LEXICAL EXTENSION

The collection of syntactic features associated with each sense (semantic reading) of a lexical item can be thought of as being divided into two mutually exclusive parts. We define the "lexical base" of an item (with respect to a given sense) as the collection of all syntactic features that determine which deep structures the item may be inserted into without violation on the deep structure level. That is, the "lexical base" determines the deep structure distribution of the item. All other syntactic information associated with each sense of a lexical item, we will call the "lexical extension" of the item with respect to that sense. The "lexical extension" will, therefore, contain syntactic features that have nothing to do with deep structure distribution and will include the Boolean function of marked exception features (R features and SD features) associated with each sense of a lexical item.

To define the notions lexical base and lexical extension is not to make a specific claim as to which features will be lexical base features and which will be lexical extension features. This is an empirical question, just as the question of which particular base rules should occur in the grammar of a language is an empirical question. Yet we know in advance that certain features will have to be in the lexical base and that others will have to be in the lexical extension of an item. For example, we know that the features [ANIMATE], [CONCRETE], [___NP], [+ANIMATE___], and so on will be lexical base features, since these features always determine deep structure distribution. And we know in advance that exception features—R features and SD features—will always be lexical extension features since they never determine deep structure distribution. After all, they are defined in terms of transformational rules, which map *given* deep structures into surface structures. Among the questionable cases will be features that denote verbal conjugation classes, noun declension classes, and grammatical gender. These will probably turn out to be lexical extension features, but the issue is by no means closed. Note that verbs do not need to be subcategorized with respect to the declensions or the grammatical genders of their subjects and objects. In Latin, for instance, there exist no verbs which must take, say, third declension objects or feminine gender subjects (as opposed to semantically female subjects). This is also true of other languages that have such features, and it may well be indicative of the fact that these are lexical extension features. However, the issue remains open with respect to these features, as well as a number of others.

Given our definitions of lexical base and lexical extension, it is possible for two lexical items to share a semantic reading and a lexical base while having different phonological properties and different lexical extensions. In fact, this is often the case with synonyms. For instance, *difficult* and *hard* share a semantic reading and a lexical base. But, as we pointed out in Section 9.1, *hard* has an irregularity that *difficult* does not have. *Hard* may not be nominalized, while *difficult* may. Thus, *hard* and *difficult* would have different lexical extensions but the same lexical base with respect to the reading that they share. Thus, the fact that *hard* (in this sense) and *difficult* are not mutually interchangeable in all environments can be attributed to a difference in their lexical extensions, rather than to a difference in their lexical bases. This is true of many synonyms and it may be true of all. It would be an interesting enterprise to see if one could constrain a linguistic theory such that lexical items with a synonymous sense always have the same lexical base with respect to that sense. If a theory with such a constraint were still empirically adequate, the constraint would then shed some light on a fact that has been noticed often. As Zellig Harris puts it, "Differences in meaning correlate highly with differences in linguistic distribution" [Harris, "Discourse Analysis," p. 378]. In a theory with the above constraint, the correlation between meaning and distribution would be exact in deep structures. The distributional differences that occur in surface structures would be due to differences in the lexical extensions of the two items, that is, they would be due to the fact that the two synonymous items may have different irregularities. We will consider this matter again in Chapter 11.

9.4 HISTORICAL CHANGE IN LEXICAL EXTENSIONS

Since lexical extensions vary substantially from person to person, it should not be surprising that even those that are shared by the great bulk of the English-speaking population should change from generation to generation. The most striking and best documented occurrences of such changes are those that have resulted in the introduction of new words into the vocabularies of most English speakers, or in the loss of old words. Many traditional grammarians as well as structural linguists have remarked on a type of lexical change in which new words patterned on old ones have been introduced into the language. The process is called "back-formation," and is usually discussed under the rubric of change by *analogy*.

Leonard Bloomfield [*Language*, pp. 415–416] cites *act*, *afflict*, and *separate* as words introduced into English by back-formation. He points out that if these verbs had been borrowed directly from Latin or French, they would not have had a -*t* ending. He concludes that the substantives *action, affliction,* and *separation* were borrowed instead, and that the corresponding verbs were later formed by analogy with a model like

> *communion:* To commune.

This conclusion is corroborated by the fact that the *Oxford English Dictionary (O.E.D.)* cites the nouns as appearing in our records at an earlier time than the corresponding verbs. As a modern example, Bloomfield gives *elocute,* a back-formation from *elocution.* He might have given an example of a more common word, *edit,* a fairly recent back-formation from *editor.*

Suppose that the words *act, afflict,* and *separate* did not exist in English today, but that *action, affliction,* and *separation* did exist. By the arguments given in Section 6.4, we would have to set up the verbs as hypothetical lexical items and mark each as being an absolute exception to NOMINALIZATION, each of them having to meet the SD of that rule. Although the verbs could never appear as verbs in the surface structure of any sentence, they would appear as verbs in the deep structure. In a sense, the verbs would be in the language, although their irregular properties represented in their lexical extensions would forbid them from appearing overtly as verbs.

Now suppose that these verbs were to enter the language suddenly. To describe the change, we would not have to add anything to the lexicon. Instead, we would have to *delete* the restriction that these verbs had to meet the structural description of the nominalization transformation. That is, we would be simplifying the lexicon, not making it more complex. This makes sense, since the language is somewhat more regular after these verbs appear than it was before. In terms of theoretical apparatus we have so far added to the theory of grammar, we can look upon back-formation as a type of change in the lexical extension of an item—and, in fact, a simplification of the lexical extension.

The verb *to aggress,* which we discussed in Section 9.2, is a good example of a back-formation that has turned up in the speech of a number of people at various times in the history of the language. The *O.E.D.* gives several citations for *aggress,* all more than a century old, and adds the touching remark: "the verb, though little used, is strictly in accordance with analogy." The *O.E.D.* will even, on occasion, mention hypothetical verbs. It lists *abluted* as "the past participle of *ablute."

In Section 6.4 we argued that a number of verbs had to be listed as hypothetical lexical items in order to account for certain derived forms of those verbs and for our intuitions about them. Many of these have actually appeared as back-formations at various times in the history of the language. A number of them were common verbs for a long period of time. Among these are *to bene-fact, to plumb, to poetize, to purpose, to consternate, to constern, to thieve, to critique,* and *to king. Webster's Third* lists *benefact* as a recent back-formation and claims that it is now in use. The *O.E.D.* cites *to plumb* as a verb that has appeared at various times. It does *not* cite it as being obsolete or archaic in the usage "to work in lead as a plumber." *Webster's Third* still considers it in current usage. *Webster's* also lists *to critique* as being current, and the *O.E.D.* gives as a citation from as long ago as 1751: "The worst ribaldry of Aristophanes shall be critiqued and commented on." *To thieve* is listed in *Webster's* as currently in use. The *O.E.D.* notes that the verb *thieve* dropped out of the language and came back in much later ("the verb is rare in O.E., after which it does not appear until the 17th century"). The *O.E.D.* lists *to king* as being rare in the sense "to rule over, or govern, as a king." It cites Shakespeare's use of the verb (*Henry V,* II, iv, 26: "Shee [France] is so badly King'd, Her Sceptre so phantastically borne"). It also quotes Bailey in 1839: "Why mad'st Thous not one spirit, like the sun, to king the world?" *To constern* is given in the *O.E.D.* as being rare, but *to consternate* is cited as being common. *To purpose* and *to poetize* are also cited in the *O.E.D.* as being common, and *Webster's* lists both as currently in use.

Considering that lexical extensions vary substantially from person to person and are apparently subject to considerable change, it is not at all surprising that verbs like those mentioned above have come into and subsequently fallen out of the language as they have.

10 HYPOTHETICAL CAUSATIVES AND INCHOATIVES

10.1 CAUSATIVES

Webster's Third International Dictionary lists the following among its entries for the words *persuade, persuasion, convince,* and *conviction:*

> *persuade:* To bring (oneself or another) to belief, certainty, or conviction.
> *persuasion:* A view held with complete assurance (example: "holding the persuasion that they could not fail").

> *convince:* To bring to or cause to have belief, acceptance, or conviction.
> *conviction:* A strong persuasion or belief.

Putting aside the other meanings of these words, let us consider how the above entries for *persuade* and *persuasion* and for *convince* and *conviction* might be related to one another. Let us also put aside the interesting question of the relationship of the phonological forms of the words to one another and concentrate on the syntactic issues involved. In the senses given above, *conviction* and *persuasion* are essentially synonymous, each meaning "a strong belief." Since the two cases are parallel, we will consider only *persuasion.*

In Section 5.12, we pointed out that *belief* is an objective nominal, derived from the verb *to believe,* and that *our belief* is derived from the abstract structure underlying "that which we believe." Since objective nominalization (OBJ-NOM) is a minor rule, *believe* must contain the feature: [m R(OBJ-NOM)]. Now, suppose we set up a hypothetical lexical item with the following properties: its phonological form is exactly that of *persuade*. Its meaning is "to believe strongly," which we will represent as: ⟨BELIEVE⟩. It is an absolute exception to the objective nominal transformation, that is, it contains the features: [m SD(OBJ-NOM)] and [m R(OBJ-NOM)]. This means that it can occur as fully grammatical only in a derivation in which it has undergone the objective nominal transformation. And it must take the affix *-ion*. We will assume that this affix is added on by a rule, and will indicate the unpredictability of the affix by the feature [m R(-ion)]. (This assumption will have no effect on our argument.) The lexical item we have constructed will, with irrelevant details omitted, look like the following:

(10-1)

   persuade and ⟨BELIEVE⟩ and [m SD(OBJ-NOM)]
      and [m R(OBJ-NOM)] and [m R(-ion)]

This lexical item can occur as grammatical only in derivations in which it has undergone OBJ-NOM and turns up as the objective nominal *persuasion* meaning "a strong belief." This is one possible way of representing *persuasion* in the above sense in the lexicon.

Now let us construct another hypothetical lexical item. It will contain the same phonological form as (10-1) and will also have the lexical meaning ⟨BELIEVE⟩. But its lexical extension will be somewhat different. It will be an absolute exception to the causative transformation [see Section 5.16]. That is, it will contain the feature [m SD(CAUSATIVE)]. Since CAUSATIVE is a minor rule, it will also contain the feature [m R(CAUSATIVE)]. This lexical item would have the following form:

(10-2)

   persuade and ⟨BELIEVE⟩ and [m SD(CAUSATIVE)]
      and [m R(CAUSATIVE)]

This lexical item will occur as fully grammatical only in derivations in which it has undergone the causative transformation. Of course, it will meet the structural description of the causative transformation only if it occurs in the following configuration:

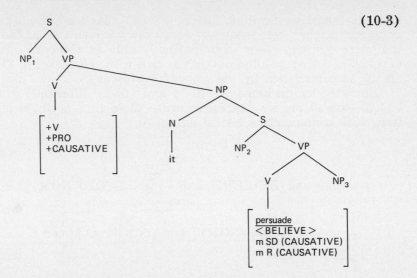

(10-3)

This configuration would underlie such sentences as: *John persuaded Bill that Harry left.*

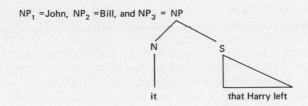

NP_1 =John, NP_2 =Bill, and NP_3 = NP

After CAUSATIVE and IT-DELETION apply, the derived structure would be:

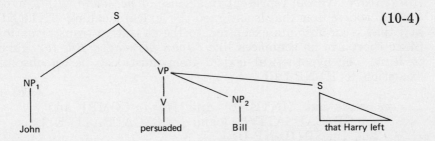

(10-4)

Thus, (10-2) is one possible way of representing *persuade* in the lexicon. Note that the lexical reading of *persuade* would not contain the causative meaning, "bring about," that we associate with *persuade*. Rather, this meaning would always result from the fact that *persuade* can occur grammatically only in the configuration of (10-3). As we pointed out in Section 5.16 the meaning "bring about" is contributed by the causative pro-verb.

Since the lexical items of (10-1) and (10-2) differ only in their lexical extensions, we can incorporate them into a single lexical item with a disjunctive lexical extension.

(10-5)

$$
\begin{array}{l}
\textit{persuade} \text{ and } \langle\text{BELIEVE}\rangle \text{ and } \Big[\ [\text{m SD(OBJ-NOM)}] \\
\qquad \text{and } [\text{m R(OBJ-NOM)}] \text{ and } [\text{m R(-ion)}] \ \Big] \ \text{ or } \\
\qquad \Big[[\text{m SD(CAUSATIVE)}] \text{ and } [\text{m R(CAUSATIVE)}] \Big]
\end{array}
$$

Through a lexical representation of this sort we can show the relationship between the senses of *persuade* and *persuasion* given above. In this representation, they are both derived from a single sense of a single lexical item, but the difference in the meaning and distribution of the words is due to the highly irregular lexical extension of (10-5). It is hard to see how one can represent the relationship between these words in any other way.

The sense of *persuade* that we represented in (10-2) was that of *John persuaded Bill that Harry left*. Note that *persuade* must take a *that*-complement in this sense. When *persuade* takes a *for-to*-complement, it has an entirely different sense, namely "to bring or cause someone to intend to do something," as in *John persuaded Bill to leave*. We can represent this sense of *persuade* with a hypothetical lexical item that is assigned the lexical meaning ⟨INTEND⟩ and that is an absolute exception to the causative transformation. Since there are no sentences like *John persuaded Bill for Harry to leave*, our hypothetical lexical item must also be an absolute exception to ID-NP-DEL.

(10-6)

$$
\begin{array}{l}
\textit{persuade} \text{ and } \langle\text{INTEND}\rangle \text{ and } [\textit{for-to}\text{-COMP}] \text{ and } \\
[\text{m SD(CAUSATIVE)}] \text{ and } [\text{m R(CAUSATIVE)}] \\
\text{and } [\text{m SD(ID-NP-DEL)}]
\end{array}
$$

The deep structure that would underlie *John persuaded Harry to leave* would, under such an analysis, be:

(10-7)

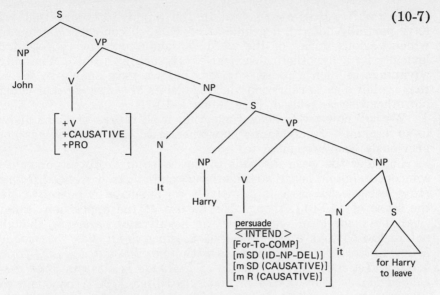

After ID-NP-DEL, IT-DEL, and CAUSATIVE have applied, the derived structure would be:

(10-8)

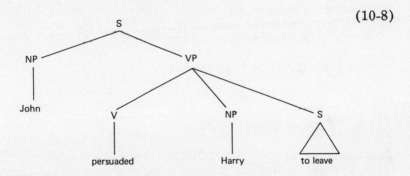

We can now represent both senses of *persuade* in a single lexical item, by combining (10-5) and (10-6):

(10-9)

persuade and $\Big[\Big[$ ⟨BELIEVE⟩ and [*that*-COMP] and

[lexical extension of (10-5)]$\Big]$ or $\Big[$⟨INTEND⟩ and

[*for-to*-COMP] and [lexical extension of (10-6)]$\Big]\Big]$

So far, we have shown that in the linguistic theory that we have partially defined, a grammar of English could be written in which various senses of the word *persuade* could be represented lexically by a hypothetical lexical entry such as (10-9). The only advantage of such a representation that we have shown so far is that it allows us to represent various senses of *persuade* that could not otherwise be related. [See Remark 10-1.]

We will now try to show that other such representations allow us to account for a syntactic phenomenon in English that has not previously been accounted for.

Consider the word *dissuade* in the sense of "to bring or cause someone to intend not to do something" as in *John dissuaded Harry from leaving. Dissuade* is intuitively an opposite of *persuade* [in the sense of (10-6)], though the nature of the opposition is not clear. *Dissuade* is in some sense the negative of *persuade,* though not in the obvious sense of negation, since *John didn't persuade Harry to leave* is not synonymous with *John dissuaded Harry from leaving.* Yet the negative quality of *dissuade* is clear in *John dissuaded Harry from seeing* anyone. As Klima [1964] has pointed out, *any* is extremely restricted in English. *Any* can occur only in sentences that contain questions, "if-then" constructions, certain modals, words like *scarcely* or *only,* or negatives. In sentences that contain negatives, but not any other conditioning environment for *any, any* may occur only *after* the verb in the sentence. It may not occur in subject position. Thus, we can get

   a. John didn't see anyone. (10-10)

but not

   b. *Anyone didn't see John.

This condition is quite general throughout the language, with certain apparent exceptions, among them *dissuade*. Since *dissuade* is inherently negative, we would correctly predict that we would get sentences like

   John dissuaded Harry from seeing *any*one. (10-11)

However, one would also predict the occurrence of the following sentence:

   *John dissuaded *any*one from seeing Harry. (10-12)

But *any,* unpredictably, may not occur with the (surface) direct object of *dissuade,* unless, of course, *dissuade* also undergoes normal negation:

John didn't dissuade anyone from seeing Harry.   (10-13)

We can account for the nonoccurrence of (10-12) and for the relation between *dissuade* and *persuade* if we hypothesize the following lexical item for *dissuade*. It will be negative in the ordinary sense and will, like the corresponding sense of *persuade,* be assigned the lexical reading ⟨INTEND⟩. The resultant lexical meaning will therefore be "to not intend." Thus, it will be the ordinary negative of the lexical representation of *persuade* (10-6). Like its opposite, *dissuade* will also be an absolute exception to the causative transformation and to ID-NP-DEL. Thus, we would have the following lexical representation for *dissuade:*

(10-14)

    dissuade and ⟨INTEND⟩ and [NEGATIVE] and
    [from-*ing*-COMP] and [m SD(CAUSATIVE)] and
    [m R(CAUSATIVE)] and [m SD(ID-NP-DEL)]

The deep structure underlying *John dissuaded Harry from leaving* would be:

(10-15)

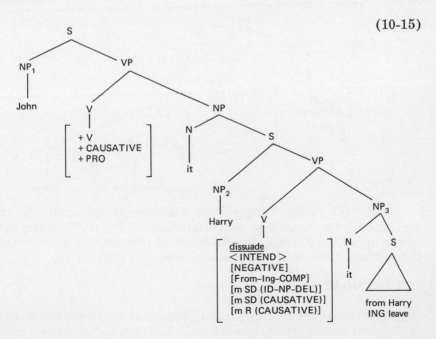

After the application of ID-NP-DEL, IT-DEL, and CAUSA-TIVE, the derived structure would be:

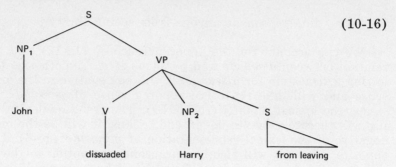

(10-16)

Note that the derived direct object of *dissuade* in (10-16) is the underlying subject of *dissuade* in (10-15). The rule which produces *any* after a negative applies cyclically, from the most deeply embedded S to the highest S. If a deep structure like (10-15) is given as input to a transformational cycle containing this rule, the rule, on the second pass of the cycle, will apply to the subtree:

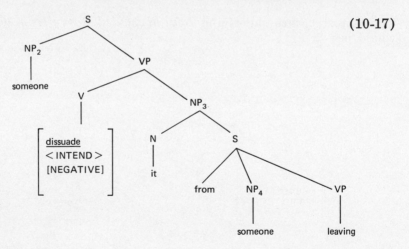

(10-17)

Since NP$_2$ is the "subject" of *dissuade* at this point in the derivation, *some* cannot be converted to *any*. Since NP$_2$ ultimately winds up as the surface direct object of *dissuade*, it follows that the surface direct object of *dissuade* may not contain *any*.

10.2 INCHOATIVES

Consider the words *kill*, *die*, and *dead*. What do these words have in common and how are they related? *Kill* means "to cause (someone) to die." Thus, we can look upon *kill* as having the same lexical meaning as *die*, but to be an absolute exception to the causative transformation. But what about *die* itself? How is it related to *dead? Die* essentially means "to come to be dead." Thus, we can consider *die* as having the same lexical meaning as *dead* and to be an absolute exception to the inchoative transformation [see Section 5.15]. We can represent *die* in the lexicon as follows:

(10-18)

> *die* and ⟨DEAD⟩ and [m SD(INCHOATIVE)] and
> [m R(INCHOATIVE)]

The deep structure underlying *John died* would then be:

(10-19)

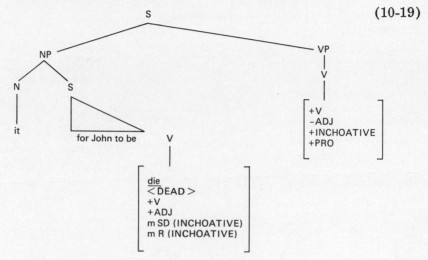

The derivation would proceed as in tree diagrams (5-19) through (5-23). The derived structure would be:

(10-20)

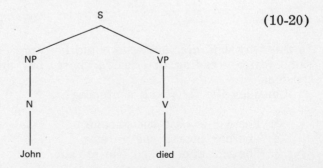

If we represent *kill* as having the same lexical meaning as *die*, but as being an absolute exception to the causative transformation as well, we would have the following lexical item:

(10-21)

kill and ⟨DEAD⟩ and [m R(INCHOATIVE)] and
   [m SD(CAUSATIVE)] and [m R(CAUSATIVE)]

The deep structure underlying *John killed Bill* would then be:

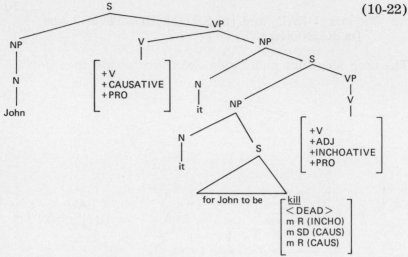

(10-22)

The derived structure would be:

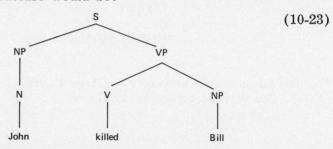

(10-23)

In this way, *kill, die,* and *dead* could be represented as having the
same lexical reading and lexical base, but different lexical extensions.

Consider the following sentences:

1. The car is near the garage.   (10-24)
2. The car neared the garage.
3. The car approached the garage.

Near in 1 is usually analyzed as a preposition. Yet phrases such as
the car's nearness to the garage would seem to indicate that *near*
is an adjective, since it can be nominalized and can take the adjective ending *-ness.* If we assume that *near* in 1 is a transitive

adjective, as it seems that we must, then we can relate 1 and 2 in a very natural way: we can derive 2 from an underlying form containing 1 by the inchoative transformation. The underlying structure of 2 would then be:

(10-25)

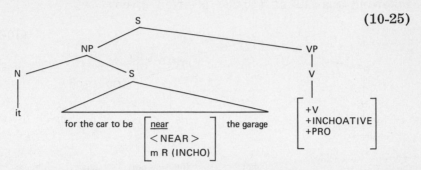

The derivation of 2 would then be parallel to the diagrams (5-19) through (5-23). Since INCHOATIVE is a minor rule, *near* would have to contain the feature [m R(INCHOATIVE)]. Now consider Sentence 3. 3 is synonymous with 2, and the verb *to approach* seems to be synonymous with the verb *to near* in 2. Since the verb *to near* in 2 must be derived via the inchoative transformation from the adjective *near* in order to relate 1 and 2, it does not seem unreasonable to derive *approach* in a parallel way from a hypothetical lexical item with the same lexical meaning as the adjective *near*. Thus, the lexical representation for *approach* might be:

(10-26)

approach and ⟨NEAR⟩ and [m R(INCHOATIVE)]
    and [m SD(INCHOATIVE)]

Thus the deep structure of 3 would be:

(10-27)

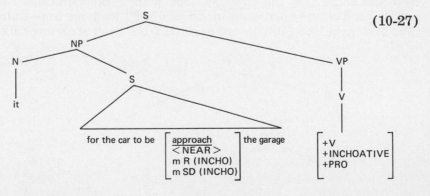

Before proceeding, we ought to counter an obvious argument against considering *near* an adjective. Consider the sentence

John shot Bill near the house.   (10-28)

In (10-28) *near* is usually analyzed as a preposition and *near the house* as a locative prepositional phrase modifying *shot Bill*. The following analysis of (10-28) is often given:

                                                                  (10-29)

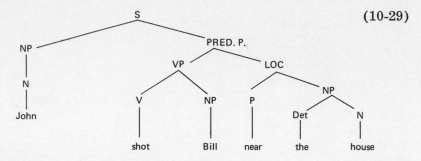

But such an analysis cannot explain how we understand the question:

Did John shoot Bill near the house? (with normal   (10-30)
intonation)

It is normally the case in questions that the uppermost VP (or perhaps the *entire* PRED. P.—if such a node exists) is what is questioned. Thus in *Does John like ice cream?* a *No* answer asserts that John does not like ice cream. In *Did John shoot Bill?* (normal intonation), a *No* answer asserts that John's shooting of Bill did not take place. However, in (10-30) what is being questioned is *not* whether or not the shooting took place. It is assumed that the shooting *did* take place, and what is being questioned is the location of the event. A *No* answer to (10-30) only denies that it was near the house that the shooting took place. Considerations such as this [and others mentioned in Appendix F] lead one to postulate that sentences like (10-28) are derived from deep structures like:

                                                                  (10-31)

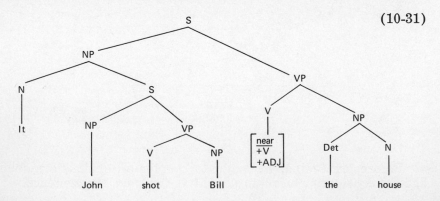

Structures like (10-31) underlie not only sentences like (10-28), but also sentences like (10-32).

It was near the house that John shot Bill.   (10-32)

Note that the negative of (10-28), namely,

John didn't shoot Bill near the house.   (10-33)

is synonymous with

It was not near the house that John shot Bill.   (10-34)

(10-33) does not deny that the shooting took place, but only denies that it was near the house. Note that (10-33) is not synonymous with the nonsentence:

*It was near the house that John didn't shoot Bill.   (10-35)

The nonoccurrence of (10-35) is due to the fact (however it is to be represented formally) that one cannot assert the location of an event which did not occur. These considerations would lead us to believe that the *not* of (10-33) is associated in the deep structure of that sentence with the VP *near the house* in (10-31) and not with the VP *shoot Bill*.

Although this by no means proves that *near* is an adjective, it does show that the existence of sentences like (10-28) is irrelevant to the question.

Consider the following sentences:

1. a. John is in the room.   (10-36)
   b. John entered the room.
2. a. John is out of the room.
   b. John left the room.

In and *out* are intuitively felt to be opposites in some sense. *Enter* and *leave* are opposites in a similar sense. And *enter* is related to *in* in the same way as *leave* is related to *out*. Moreover, each of the above b sentences entails its corresponding a sentence.

We can account for these facts if we assume that *in* and *out*, like *near*, are transitive adjectives. This makes some sense since *in* and *out* in (10-36) have independent cognitive content and can be looked at semantically as two-place predicates relating *John* and *the room*. By the same arguments that we used with *near*, all other occurrences of "locative" *in* and *out* can be reduced to the above case in underlying analyses. Thus, it is not implausible to consider these words as transitive adjectives. If we do so we can set up the following hypothetical lexical items for *enter* and *leave*.

(10-37)

    enter and ⟨IN⟩ and [+V] and [+STATIVE] and
    [m SD(INCHOATIVE)] and [m R(INCHOATIVE)]

    leave and ⟨OUT⟩ and [+V] and [+STATIVE] and
    [m SD(INCHOATIVE)] and [m R(INCHOATIVE)]

Like *approach, enter* and *leave* can be considered absolute exceptions to the inchoative transformation, with *enter* having the meaning of *in* and *leave* having the meaning of *out*. Thus, *John entered the room* would have the following underlying structure:

(10-38)

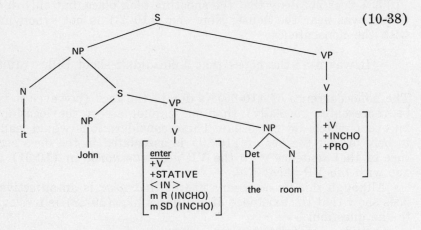

Note that the embedded S in (10-38) is semantically equivalent to the underlying structure of *John is in the room*. In this way we can explain the fact that in (10-36) 1.b entails 1.a.

    Consider the following:

    1. a. John has the book.   (10-39)
       b. John doesn't have the book.
    2. a. John gained the book.
       b. John lost the book.

In these sentences, 2.a entails 1.a and 2.b entails 1.b. *Gain* and *lose* are opposites in the same way as *have* and *not have* are. And *gain* is related to *have* as *lose* is related to *not have*. We can represent these facts by considering *gain* and *lose* as absolute exceptions to the inchoative transformation and by setting up appropriate lexical items in which *gain* has the lexical meaning "have" and *lose* has the lexical meaning "not have."

(10-40)

gain and ⟨HAVE⟩ and [+V] and [+STATIVE]
and [m SD(INCHOATIVE)] and [m R(INCHOATIVE)]

lose and ⟨HAVE⟩ and [NEGATIVE] and [+V]
and [+STATIVE] and [m SD(INCHOATIVE)]
and [m R(INCHOATIVE)]

The deep structure underlying *John lost the book* would then be:

(10-41)

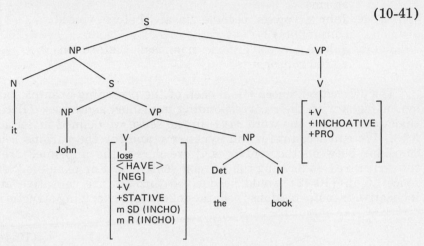

Note that the embedded S is semantically equivalent to the deep structure of *John doesn't have the book.*

Gain and *lose* are typical examples of one change on the one hand and a change in a reverse direction on the other. Given the above representations for these words, we can represent the notion of "reverse change" in terms of the more primitive notions of "inchoative" and "negative." A more complicated example is the following:

1. a. John activated the bomb.   (10-42)
   b. John deactivated the bomb.
2. a. John nasalizes his vowels (when he imitates a Frenchman).
   b. John denasalizes his vowels (when he imitates an actor).
1'. a. John caused the bomb to become active.
   b. John caused the bomb to become inactive.
2'. a. John makes his vowels become nasal (when he imitates a Frenchman).
   b. John makes his vowels become nonnasal (when he imitates an actor).

1. a. The bomb activated (when the fire reached it). *(10-43)*
   b. The bomb deactivated (during the rainstorm).
2. a. John's vowels nasalize (before voiced conso-
      nants).
   b. John's vowels denasalize (before unvoiced
      consonants).
1'. a. The bomb became active (when the fire reached
       it).
    b. The bomb became inactive (during the rain-
       storm).
2'. a. John's vowels become nasal (before voiced
       consonants).
    b. John's vowels become nonnasal (before un-
       voiced consonants).

The primed sentences (') in each of the preceding examples are
synonymous with their corresponding unprimed sentences. (Recall
that we are using the word *cause* in the sense we defined in Section
5.16.) We can account for this synonymy and for the various relationships between the sentences if we derive the unprimed from
the structures underlying the primed sentences. For example, Sentence 1.b in (10-42) would be derived through the causative and
inchoative transformations from the following underlying structure:

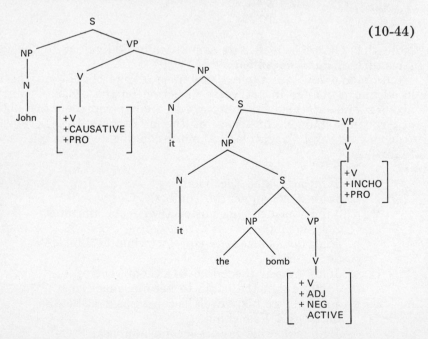

(10-44)

Note that the structure starting with the second highest S would
underlie Sentence 1.b in (10-43).

Using such representations we can derive reverse processes and their causatives in a very natural way. We can also state a very simple rule in English for the addition of the prefix *de-* in the above examples: *de-* is added to adjectives that are negative and that undergo the inchoactive transformation.

10.3 JUSTIFICATION

When we incorporated the notion of absolute exception into our theory of grammar, we increased the class of possible lexical items defined by the theory to include the hypothetical ones discussed in this section. Although we have shown that causatives and inchoatives can be adequately represented by the use of absolute exception features, we certainly have not ruled out other possible ways of representing them. What we have shown is that, by using the independently motivated notion of an absolute exception and the independently motivated causative and inchoative transformations, we can describe many facts about causatives and inchoatives. We can also simplify our theory of grammar by eliminating the possible primitive notion "reverse process." Other theories may exist in which it is possible to account for all of these facts with equal generality and to make the same simplification. To my knowledge, no other such theory has yet been proposed. [See Remark 10-2.]

11 SOME SPECULATIONS ON UNIVERSAL GRAMMAR

Because research in the transformational grammar of various languages has turned up base components which look more or less alike, speculation has grown that the base components of all natural languages may turn out to be identical—at least in the grammatical relations that they define. That is, the base component, rather than being an idiosyncratic part of the particular grammars of individual languages, may be part of the theory of language, namely, that which characterizes natural language and that which every child has inherent knowledge of prior to learning his native language.

Similar speculation has centered on the possibility that the semantic components may also be universal. In view of the paucity of our knowledge in these areas, both proposals must remain in the realm of speculation for some time to come. Yet they form empirical hypotheses of considerable interest, and point the way to what may be useful research.

Of course, the proposal that the base component is universal is totally empty in the absence of any other strong constraints on the form of grammar. However, given particular constraints on the form of transformational rules and on other aspects of grammar, it becomes an empirical question as to whether a theory of language constrained in such a way will define adequate grammars for two languages, such that those grammars have the same base component. For instance, given the constraints on the form of grammar that we have proposed so far—(1) that arbitrary subcategorization be ruled out, (2) that grammatical transformations not be permitted to refer to particular lexical items, and (3) that possible exceptions be defined in the way that we have specified—it may be the case that these constraints are not compatible with the hypothesis of a universal base component (if, indeed, they are compatible with one another). On the other hand, if these independently motivated constraints were to turn out to be compatible with the universal base hypothesis, it would be an interesting fact about natural language.

The empirical hypothesis of a universal base component and a universal semantic component—if they can be maintained together with well-motivated constraints on the form of grammar—could help explain such phenomena as a child's ability to learn his native language. If it could be assumed that the child had in advance a built-in mechanism that defined the set of possible deep structures with which he had to associate the abstract representations that he perceived of the speech sounds that reached his ears, then the child's job of formulating a theory to match surface structures with deep structures might be conceived of as being within the realm of the possible. The assumption of a fixed base structure would greatly limit the number of grammars defined by the theory, that is, the number of grammars available to the child. As things now stand in the study of grammar, the number of grammars defined by our present theories is so large that it is inconceivable that a child could choose among them and find an adequate one within the short span of time in which he actually learns his native language.

In Section 9.3, we considered another possible constraint on the grammars of natural languages: that lexical bases be predictable from the semantic readings of lexical items. By "semantic reading" we mean only one of the many senses of a lexical item: in Fodor-Katz [1964] terms, a single path through the tree of semantic markers. We could, of course, consider a stronger hypothesis—that each feature of the lexical base associated with a sense of a lexical item be predictable from a single semantic marker of that sense. For example, the syntactic feature [+ANIMATE] might be predicted from the semantic marker ⟨ANIMAL⟩, or the syntactic feature [−STATIVE] for verbs might be predicted from the semantic marker ⟨ACTIVITY⟩. Such a hypothesis would state, among other things, that if two lexical items had partially similar lexical meanings, and if the similarity lay in those semantic markers like ⟨ANIMAL⟩ from which syntactic features could be predicted, then the two lexical items would have partially similar lexical bases. This may well be a feasible position, but we will not consider it here. We mention it only to distinguish it from the weaker hypothesis which is under consideration—that the *collection* of the features in the lexical base associated with a single sense of a lexical item is predictable from the *collection* of semantic markers that make up that sense. [See Remark 11-1.]

This hypothesis—which we will call the "lexical base hypothesis"—is, of course, not obviously true and could be falsified. Observe that the feature [__NP] must necessarily be a possible lexical base feature, no matter how narrowly one construes the notion "lexical base." Therefore, one way in which the lexical base hypothesis could be falsified would be for someone to find two synonyms, one of which was transitive and the other intransitive (in the deep structure, of course). It is hard to imagine what such a pair of synonyms would be like (since this phenomenon does not appear to occur in natural language), but it is certainly logically possible that such a phenonenon could exist.

Note that since the features of the lexical base are in part introduced in the base component (inherent features) and in part defined with respect to the base component (contextual features), such a hypothesis can make sense only within the context of a theory in which the base component is universal. Since the lexical base hypothesis must assume the universal base hypothesis, it is at least as likely, a priori, to be incompatible with other constraints on the form of grammar. It would be an interesting fact should it turn out to be compatible with such constraints.

Whether or not the lexical base hypothesis should be maintained is at this time an open question which, for lack of knowledge, can hardly be sensibly debated. What we would like to do is to point out what some of the consequences of this hypothesis would be— the facts it could explain, the claims it would make, and the sort of research it might lead to.

As we pointed out in Section 9.3, one immediate consequence of the lexical base hypothesis would be that synonyms would have the same lexical bases—that is, they would have the same deep structure distribution and any differences in surface structure distribution would be due to differences in their lexical extensions. This would account for our intuition, which has long been articulated by grammarians, that meaning in some sense determines distribution, though it by no means does so precisely.

In a theory in which the lexical base hypothesis is assumed, we can present certain formal arguments to account for our intuitions. Consider the following:

1. a. Writing papers is difficult for me.   (11-1)
   b. Writing papers is hard for me.
2. a. My difficulty at writing papers
   b. *My hardness at writing papers

As we observed in Section A.6, FLIP and NOMINALIZATION are mutually exclusive. Therefore, in verbs that can undergo FLIP, the underlying subject shows up in the genitive when NOMINALIZATION applies. We can explain the relationship between 1.a and 2.a if we assume that FLIP has occurred in the derivation of 1.a, but that, as one would expect, it has not occurred in the derivation of 2.a. There does not seem to be any other well-motivated way of explaining the relationship between 1.a and 2.a. Thus, 2.a shows that I is the underlying subject of 1.a, even though it appears in object position. However, because of the nonoccurrence of 2.b, we cannot make the same argument for *hard* as we did for *difficult*. But if we assume the lexical base hypothesis, we can argue that since *hard* and *difficult* are synonymous in 1, they have the same lexical base. We then could argue, on this basis, that I is the underlying subject of 1.b, since it is in 1.a. This would reflect our intuition that 1.a displays the same grammatical relations as 1.b. Since our intuitions about lexical synonymy are usually better than our intuitions about underlying grammatical relations, the lexical base hypothesis—if it could be maintained—would permit us to use the former to gain insight about the latter.

The lexical base hypothesis would make claims not only about synonyms within a language, but about synonyms across languages. Thus, if a lexical item in Language A is synonymous with one in Language B, the lexical base hypothesis would claim that the two items have the same lexical base. Thus, grammatical information about one language would be quite relevant to the grammatical analysis of another language. This would be completely contrary to the methodological theories (though not the practices) of most modern linguists, including transformational grammarians. Yet, in this case, the lexical base hypothesis would explain a very deep fact about language (which was pointed out by Postal in personal communication). When an adult learns a foreign language and is taught what a new word means, there are certain facts about that word that he knows immediately and that he does not have to be taught. An English speaker learning the Mohawk verb meaning *to try* does not have to be taught *not* to say the Mohawk equivalents of **The idea tried the rock* or **The rock tried to go* or **That Bill went there tried*. Instead, he knows automatically that a verb meaning *to try* must take an animate subject and an abstract object. This is the sort of thing that a language teacher never has to teach, and it is something that one will never find in a pedagogical grammar. One simply does not have to "learn" that the Turkish word for *table* is inanimate and concrete; one knows it in advance, and it is inconceivable that it could be otherwise. Someone (for instance, the author) who does not know a word of Hungarian can be completely certain that the Hungarian verb meaning *to hate* takes animate subjects and that the Hungarian verb meaning *to believe* takes animate subjects and abstract objects. This is a very deep fact about language which the lexical base hypothesis could explain.

Note that the lexical base hypothesis does not make a claim about which features may compose a lexical base, just as the universal base hypothesis is quite distinct from a proposal that a particular set of base rules is universal. Indeed, any proposal that lexical bases may be composed of a given set of features would depend strongly on a proposal for a particular set of base rules, and vice versa. Because the set of base rules and the features of possible lexical bases are intimately bound up with one another, it is quite conceivable that evidence about syntactic features of lexical bases could shed some light on what the universal base rules should be (if they exist). [See Remark 11-2.]

APPENDIXES

A ADJECTIVES AND VERBS

We will try to present a case for the plausibility of the assertion that adjectives and verbs are members of a single lexical category (which we will call VERB) and that they differ only by a single syntactic feature (which we will call ADJECTIVAL).

Of the arguments given below, 1, 4, 5, 7, and 9 were worked out by Paul Postal and by the author, working independently. Arguments 2, 6, and 8 are due solely to Postal; 3 was pointed out by Lester Rice.

A.1 GRAMMATICAL RELATIONS

There are a great many pairs of sentences—in which one contains a verb where the other contains an adjective—that are understood in the same way. For example,

1. a. I regret that.   (A-1)
   b. I am sorry about that.
2. a. I like jazz.
   b. I am fond of jazz.
3. a. I forgot that fact.
   b. I was oblivious of that fact.
4. a. I know about that.
   b. I am cognizant of that.
   b'. I am aware of that.

There are other pairs of the same sort, where the adjective and verb seem to be the same lexical item.

1. a. I desire that.   (A-2)
   b. I am desirous of that.

115

2. a. John hopes that peace will come soon.
   b. John is hopeful that peace will come soon.
3. a. I fear that the Dodgers will win.
   b. I am fearful that the Dodgers will win.
4. a. John considers Mary's feelings.
   b. John is considerate of Mary's feelings.
5. a. That will please John.
   b. That will be pleasing to John.
6. a. That excites me.
   b. That is exciting to me.
7. a. Our actions in the Dominican Republic appall me.
   b. Our actions in the Dominican Republic are appalling to me.
8. a. Massachusetts politics amuses me.
   b. Massachusetts politics is amusing to me.
9. a. Cigarettes harm people.
   b. Cigarettes are harmful to people.
10. a. The President's decision surprised me.
    b. The President's decision was surprising to me.

In most of the above cases, the a and b sentences differ only in that the b sentences contain *be* + adjective + preposition where the a sentences contain a verb. These differences are quite superficial. The auxiliary verb, *be,* serves only to carry the tense marker before adjectives, in just the same way as *do* carries the tense marker before verbs in negative and question sentences. Although no preposition appears after the verb in the surface structure of the a sentences, there is good reason to believe that the preposition is there on some level of analysis, since prepositions do show up when verbs are nominalized. Thus we get:

a. My fear *of* rain . . . ↔ I fear rain.   (A-3)
b. My liking *for* jazz . . . ↔ I like jazz.
c. John's desire *for* Mary . . . ↔ John desires Mary.
d. John's consideration *of* Mary's feelings . . . ↔ John considers Mary's feelings.

It appears that there is a late rule in English which drops prepositions after verbs that have not been nominalized. It is a moot question whether such prepositions appear in the deep structures of the above sentences or whether they are introducd by "spelling rules" which insert them before the object noun phrase as a kind of case marking. I will assume that the latter is the case, though this assumption will not matter in any of the following arguments. Similarly, it is not clear at present whether tense markings should be introduced as part of an auxiliary constituent or as features of verbs and adjectives, which are later inserted before the adjective or verb by spelling rules. I will assume the latter, though again the arguments to follow will be independent of this assumption.

It seems highly significant that the a and b sentences of (A-1) and (A-2) are understood in the same way and this fact seems to be a consequence of the presence of the same grammatical relationships in each pair of sentences. For example, in the sentences *I like John* and *I am fond of John, fond* seems to bear the same relation to *John* as *like* bears to *John*. And *John* seems to bear the same relation to *like* as it does to *fond*. But, in order for *like* and *fond* to be involved in the same grammatical relations, they would have to be members of the same lexical category.

Of course, just because the a and b sentences of (A-1) and (A-2) are synonymous and seem to be understood in the same way, it does not necessarily follow that the same grammatical relations hold in each pair of sentences. It might very well be the case that the semantic component of a grammar of English might have projection rules that interpret two different sets of grammatical relations as though they were identical. Thus, it might be the case that the projection rules of English interpret the following two structures in exactly the same way:

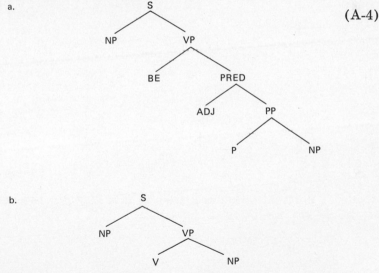

Though we do not rule this alternative out as a possibility, we would argue that the semantic component would be simpler if it had to contain only projection rules to interpret one of these structures. Still, such a simplification in the semantic component could be offset if our assumption were to hopelessly complicate the syntactic component of a grammar of English. As we will try to show below, this does not seem to be the case. We will argue that, just as we do not lose anything semantically by making this assumption, so we do not lose anything syntactically either. On the contrary, it seems that this assumption points the way to greater syntactic generalization.

We ought to present some examples of the kinds of grammatical analyses that we have in mind. We would represent the derivations of *I like John* and *I am fond of John* as in (A-5). Note that the deep structures of these sentences a.(i) and b.(i) are nearly identical.

a. (i) DEEP STRUCTURE   (A-5)

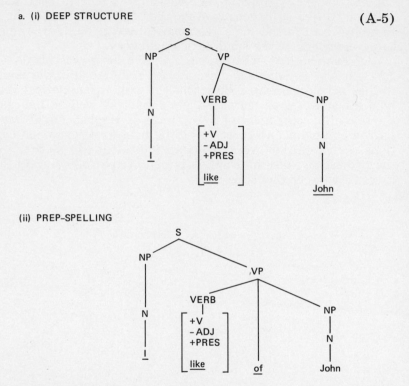

(ii) PREP-SPELLING

(Note, if nominalization occurred at this point in the derivation, we would get *my liking* of *John*.)

(iii) PREP-DELETION

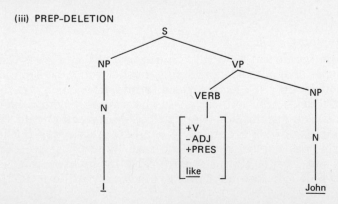

b. (i) DEEP STRUCTURE

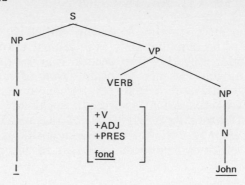

(ii) TENSE-SPELLING

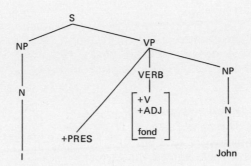

(iii) PREP-SPELLING

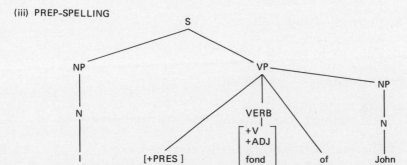

(iv) BE-ADDITION

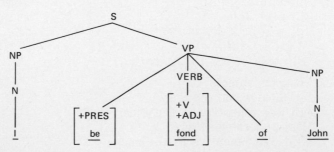

A.2 SELECTIONAL RESTRICTIONS

Perhaps the most striking syntactic similarity between adjectives
and verbs is the fact that they take almost all of the same contextual restrictions. Taking into account, as we did in the preceding
section, that the presence of *be* in front of adjectives and prepositions after them is a superficial phenomenon, we can speak of
transitive adjectives, just as we can speak of transitive verbs, as
having the feature [+__NP]. All of the adjectives in (A-1) and
(A-2) are examples. Similarly, we can speak of intransitive adjectives, just as we can speak of intransitive verbs. For example,

    a. John is alive.   (A-6)
    b. John walks.

Both have the feature [+__#].
    Moreover, adjectives and verbs can take the same kinds of
subjects and objects.

    a. Animate subject: (A-7)
       I know that fact.
       I am aware of that fact.
       *The rock knows that fact.
       *The rock is aware of that fact.

    b. Physical object subject:
       The box weighs a lot.
       The box is very heavy.
       *Sincerity weighs a lot.
       *Sincerity is very heavy.

    c. Abstract subject:
       His running away meant that we would have to
       leave.
       His running away was equivalent to treason.
       *The rock meant that we would have to leave.
       *The rock was equivalent to treason.

    d. Animate objects:
       Bill hurt John.
       Bill was brutal to John.
       *Bill hurt the rock.
       *Bill was brutal to the rock.

    e. Abstract objects:
       Bill understood the idea.
       Bill was receptive to the idea.
       *Bill understood the rock.
       *Bill was receptive to the rock.

Adjectives and verbs also take many of the same types of adverbials.

a. Time adverbials: (A-8)
They were noisy all night.
They caroused all night.
They were noisy till 4 A.M.
They caroused till 4 A.M.
They were being noisy at midnight.
They were carousing at midnight.
They are often noisy.
They often carouse.

b. Locative adverbials:
They were being noisy in the living room.
They were carousing in the living room.

c. Manner adverbials:
They were being noisy deliberately.
They were screaming deliberately.

A.3 STATIVE AND NONSTATIVE VERBS AND ADJECTIVES

Both adjectives and verbs can be subcategorized with respect to the feature STATIVE (or NONACTIVITY) and as a result, both can undergo, or fail to undergo, rules conditioned by that feature.

a. Imperative: (A-9)
Look at the picture.
*Know that Bill went there.
Don't be noisy.
*Don't be tall.

b. Do-something:
What I'm doing is looking at the picture.
*What I'm doing is knowing that Bill went there.
What I'm doing is being noisy.
*What I'm doing is being tall.

c. Progressive:
I'm looking at the picture.
*I'm knowing that Bill went there.
I'm being noisy.
*I'm being tall.

The subcategorization of these verbs and adjectives with respect to the feature STATIVE is the following:

	look at	*know*	*noisy*	*tall*
STATIVE	−	+	−	+

Note that if we do not assume that verbs and adjectives belong to the same major category, the rules that yield a, b, and c above will all have to refer to both verbs and adjectives in the same place in the structural description of each rule. That is, one term of the SD in each rule will be: $\left\{ \begin{array}{c} \text{verb} \\ \text{adjective} \end{array} \right\}$. For three rules to have the same disjunction of different major categories in their structural descriptions would be somewhat coincidental. As we shall see below, there are more than three such rules. Indeed, there are so many more that we can effectively rule out coincidence.

A.4 THE ADJECTIVE SHIFT

There are two rules in English which are necessary to derive the common adjectival construction that appears in *the tall man* from relative clauses like *the man who is tall*. The first rule, call it WH-DEL, deletes the sequence WH + PRONOUN + BE when preceded by a noun and followed by either an adjective or a verb $\left(\left\{ \begin{array}{c} \text{adjective} \\ \text{verb} \end{array} \right\} \right)$. WH-DEL will convert *the man who is tall* into *the man tall, the child who is sleeping soundly* into *the child sleeping soundly,* and *the man who is in the yard* into *the man in the yard.* Following WH-DEL, there is an obligatory rule which converts *the man tall* into *the tall man.* Call this ADJ-SHIFT. ADJ-SHIFT permutes a noun with a following adjective or verb $\left(\left\{ \begin{array}{c} \text{adjective} \\ \text{verb} \end{array} \right\} \right)$ when both are dominated by a noun phrase which immediately dominates the noun.

The following derivations result from applying WH-DEL and ADJ-SHIFT in that order.

> The man who was murdered $\Rightarrow$ the murdered man   (A-10)
> The man who is dead $\Rightarrow$ the dead man
> The child who is sleeping $\Rightarrow$ the sleeping child
> The child who is quiet $\Rightarrow$ the quiet child
> The dog that is barking $\Rightarrow$ the barking dog
> The dog that is noisy $\Rightarrow$ the noisy dog

Thus, we have examples of two more rules that apply to $\left\{ \begin{array}{c} \text{adjective} \\ \text{verb} \end{array} \right\}$.

Note, by the way, that ADJ-SHIFT as we have described it is not adequately formulated. The rule that we gave will not account for the following derivations:

> The child who is soundly sleeping $\Rightarrow$ the soundly   (A-11)
>   sleeping child
> The boy who is occasionally obnoxious $\Rightarrow$ the occa-
>   sionally obnoxious boy

Our first guess as to how these may be derived might be that instead of permuting $\begin{Bmatrix} \text{adjective} \\ \text{verb} \end{Bmatrix}$ in ADJ-SHIFT, we should permute the entire verb phrase. If this is so, it would nullify our argument that $\begin{Bmatrix} \text{adjective} \\ \text{verb} \end{Bmatrix}$ must appear in the structural description of ADJ-SHIFT. However, if we adopt this suggestion, we cannot account for the nonoccurrence of the following derivations:

> The child who is sleeping soundly $\not\Rightarrow$ *the sleeping (A-12)
>   soundly child
> The boy who is obnoxious occasionally $\not\Rightarrow$ *the ob-
>   noxious occasionally boy

To account for this phenomenon we must hypothesize that the permuted element in ADJ-SHIFT is a verb phrase that ends in $\begin{Bmatrix} \text{adjective} \\ \text{verb} \end{Bmatrix}$. In fact, we must modify this proposal to include the condition that the verb phrase must immediately dominate the final $\begin{Bmatrix} \text{adjective} \\ \text{verb} \end{Bmatrix}$ in order to account for the fact that we can have derivation a of (A-13) but not b or c of (A-13).

> a. John is a man who is hard to please $\Rightarrow$ John is a (A-13)
>   hard man to please
> b. John is a man who is able to run $\not\Rightarrow$ *John is an
>   able man to run
> c. John is a man who is able to run $\not\Rightarrow$ *John is an
>   able to run man

ADJ-SHIFT would apply to a tree of the form

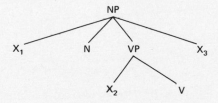

and would map such trees into trees of the form

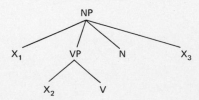

The fact that we get a but not b is due to the fact that the derived constituent structures of the two sentences are different.

a starts out in the embedded clause as:

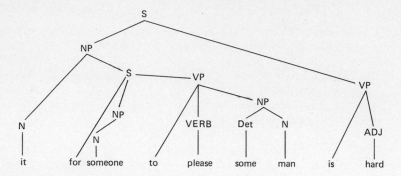

This gets transformed to:

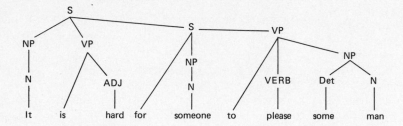

This becomes:

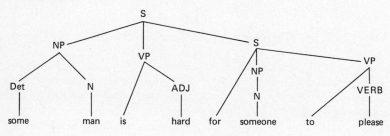

which, after the deletion of *for someone,* becomes,

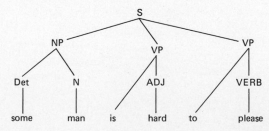

This will meet the conditions for our revised ADJ-SHIFT, after the relative clause embedding rule pronominalizes *man* and WH-DEL applies. b, on the other hand, starts out as:

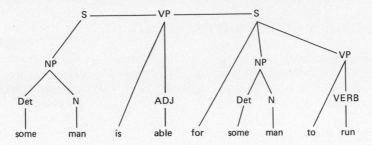

which is transformed into:

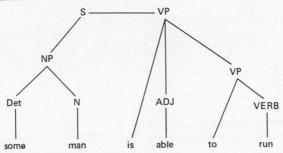

This structure will not meet the structural description of our revised ADJ-SHIFT rule, after the relative clause rule and WH-DEL apply.

A.5 NOMINALIZATIONS

Adjectives and verbs both undergo the same factive, action, and manner nominalizations. Since the structures that result from these rules look identical, it is not certain whether there is a single rule that operates to produce these structures, or whether there is a battery of separate, but partially similar, rules. If the former is the case, then there is at least one more rule in a grammar of English that refers to $\left\{ \begin{array}{l} \text{adjective} \\ \text{verb} \end{array} \right\}$. If there is more than one such rule, then our case is that much stronger.

The following are some examples of such nominalizations:

John knows that fact ⇒ John's knowledge of that (A-14)
   fact
John is cognizant of that fact ⇒ John's cognizance
   of that fact

John yelled ⇒ John's yelling
John was noisy ⇒ John's noisiness
John distrusted Bill ⇒ John's distrust of Bill
John was wary of Bill ⇒ John's wariness of Bill

A.6 SUBJECT-OBJECT INTERCHANGE

It seems necessary to postulate a transformation that interchanges the subject and object of some adjectives and verbs, in order to account for the relationships between pairs of sentences like the following:

a. What he did amused me.   (A-15)
   I was amused at what he did.
b. What he did surprised me.
   I was surprised at what he did.
c. What he had done pleased her.
   She was pleased at what he had done.
d. His explanation satisfied me.
   I was satisfied with his explanation.
e. I enjoy movies.
   Movies are enjoyable to me.

We will call this transformation FLIP. In a–d, FLIP has applied to the sentence containing the verb. In e, it has applied to the sentence containing the adjective. We know this from our intuitions about what the underlying subjects and objects are, and these intuitions are strengthened by the fact that they are mirrored in actual data, since the underlying subject-object relation is unchanged under nominalization. This is clear in the following examples.

a. My amusement at what he did   (A-16)
b. My surprise at what he did
c. Her pleasure at what he had done
d. My satisfaction with his explanation
e. My enjoyment of movies

The FLIP rule can also account for the fact that in (A-17)

a. What he had done pleased her   (A-17)
b. She liked what he had done

she seems to bear the same relation to *like* as *her* bears to *please*. We can describe this fact easily if we assume that either a or b has undergone FLIP.

From the nominalization of b,

Her liking of what he had done   (A-18)

it is clear that a, not b, has undergone FLIP.

FLIP is then another rule of English which applies to either adjectives or verbs and which must refer to $\left\{ \begin{array}{c} \text{adjective} \\ \text{verb} \end{array} \right\}$ in its structural description.

A.7 OBJECT DELETION

Object deletion is a common phenomenon in English. There is a rule which deletes indefinite direct object pronouns optionally after certain verbs. For example,

a. John is eating something $\Rightarrow$ John is eating   (A-19)
b. John is drinking something $\Rightarrow$ John is drinking

There is also a rule that optionally deletes a preposition and an indefinite pronoun after certain adjectives. For instance,

a. The movie was enjoyable to someone $\Rightarrow$ The movie   (A-20)
   was enjoyable
b. The results are suggestive of something $\Rightarrow$ The
   results are suggestive
c. The movie was objectionable to someone $\Rightarrow$ The
   movie was objectionable

Considering that the occurrence of a preposition after an adjective is a superficial feature of English [see (A-1)], then the indefinite pronouns deleted in (A-20) are actually in direct object position, and the rule that deletes them is actually the same as the rule that deletes such pronouns in (A-19). Here is another rule that applies both in the case of adjectives and verbs.

A.8 AGENT NOMINALS

Both adjectives and verbs may be transformed into agent nouns. For example,

a. She is beautiful.   (A-21)
   She is a beauty.
b. He is idiotic.
   He is an idiot.
c. John is foolish.
   John is a fool.
d. John cooks.
   John is a cook.

e. John kills men.
John is a killer of men.
f. John destroys houses.
John is a destroyer of houses.

(I assume that the adjective endings *-ful, -ic, -ish,* are added by late spelling rules onto adjectives that have not been transformed into nouns.)

Note that adverbs that modify verbs and adjectives are transformed into adjectives when the agent rule applies. For instance,

a. She is really beautiful.   (A-22)
She is a real beauty.
b. He is utterly idiotic.
He is an utter idiot.
c. John is completely foolish.
John is a complete fool.
d. John cooks well.
John is a good cook.
e. John kills men mercilessly.
John is a merciless killer of men.
f. John destroys houses professionally.
John is a professional destroyer of houses.

Thus, AGENT is another rule that applies to both adjectives and verbs.

A.9 COMPLEMENTS

Both adjectives and verbs seem to be able to take the same variety of subject, object, and predicate complements, and the same complement rules seem to apply regardless of whether an adjective or verb is present. A detailed justification of this assertion is impossible here, and though none has yet appeared in the literature, P. S. Rosenbaum [1967, Chapter 6] discusses some of the similarities between adjectives and verbal complements.

Instead, I will try to make a case for the plausibility of the assertion by presenting some examples of sentences with verb and adjective complements that seem to have the same underlying structure and seem to have undergone the same rules.

a. John wants to go.   (A-23)
John is eager to go.
b. John knew that Bill had done it.
John was aware that Bill had done it.
c. John feared that Bill would come.
John was afraid that Bill would come.

d. John can hit a ball 400 feet.
   John is able to hit a ball 400 feet.
e. John hesitated to do that.
   John was reluctant to do that.
f. It happened that John left.
   It is likely that John will leave.
g. John happened to leave.
   John is likely to leave.

A more complicated example is the following:

a. I need to know that.   (A-24)
b. It is necessary for me to know that.

Sentence a is straightforward.

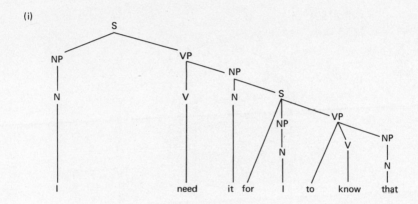

Deletion of embedded subject under identity: (ID-NP-DEL).

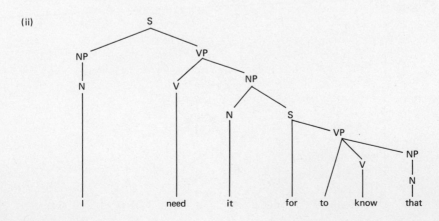

IT-DELETION

(iii)

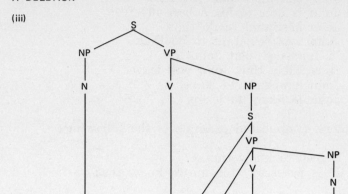

FOR-DELETION

(iv)

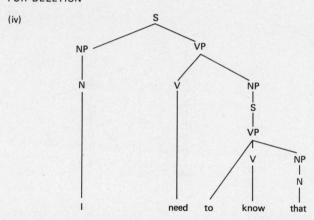

(i)

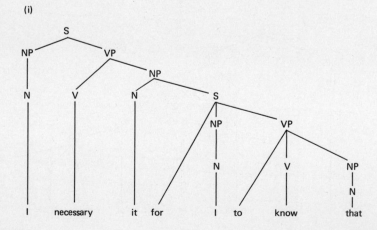

(ii) ID-NP-DEL

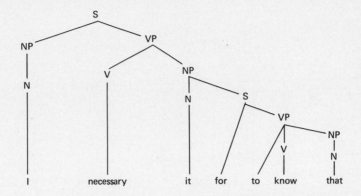

(iii) FLIP

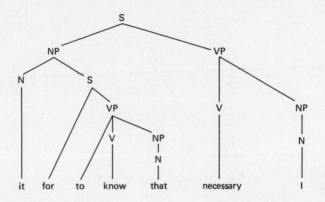

(iv) EXTRAPOSITION

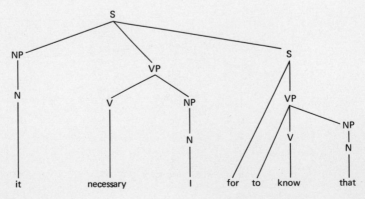

(v) FOR-DELETION

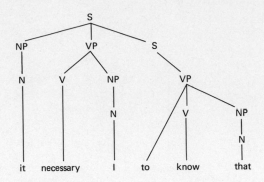

(vi) TENSE-SPELLING

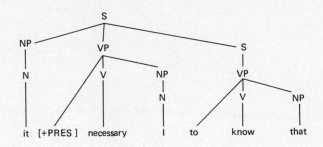

(vii) PREP-SPELLING

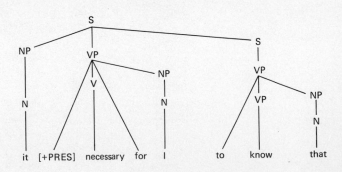

(viii) BE-ADDITION

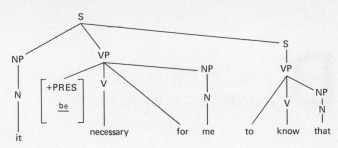

CONCLUSION

We have seen that there are at least ten very general rules of English in which adjectives and verbs are treated identically. This hardly seems accidental. If it were, we would expect to find just as many transformational rules in which verbs and nouns were treated identically—or in which nouns and adjectives were treated identically. This is not the case.

These considerations are mirrored by considerations of generality. If we postulate a single category, VERB, we will save one symbol for each occurrence of $\begin{Bmatrix} \text{adjective} \\ \text{verb} \end{Bmatrix}$ in the transformational rules of English, and so achieve some greater generality. Thus, our assertion not only simplifies the semantic component somewhat, but also does the same for the syntactic component.

B POSSIBLE BUT INCORRECT ANALYSES

The definition of a violation given in 1.51 will have to be extended somewhat. Suppose the choices of (1-4) were made in the context:

I saw the _____.

The choices would then yield:

a. I saw the rock.
and
b. I saw the boy.

Note that in this situation our conventions would mark a as containing a violation. Note too that the rules of (1-3) also generate the following complex symbols:

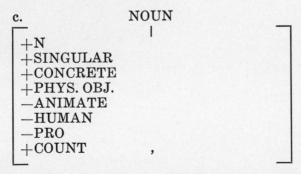

c.   NOUN
                       |
⎡ +N
  +SINGULAR
  +CONCRETE
  +PHYS. OBJ.
  −ANIMATE
  −HUMAN
  −PRO
  +COUNT   , ⎤

There will be a derivation in which c will also occur in the context *I saw the* _____, and so the grammar will also define derivations in which *rock* and *boy* are substituted for the lexical member of c.

Thus, the grammar will, in these cases, generate the terminal strings a and b, but with the grammatical features of the object noun being c rather than (1-1). In this case, our convention would mark b, not a, as containing a violation.

This may seem strange at first, but it actually makes very good sense. Remember that we required the following of a theory of grammar: Given a particular grammar and given a sentence, the theory should tell us all of the structural descriptions that the grammar assigns to that sentence (that is, all of the grammatical analyses of that sentence that are defined by the given grammar). But this does not mean that we should require the metatheory only to yield analyses that are completely correct relative to the grammar. It is also reasonable to require that the metatheory yield partially correct grammatical analyses, which are marked in the way in which they deviate from correctness. For instance, it would be incorrect to analyze *rock* in a as being animate and human, though it would be correct to analyze it as being inanimate and nonhuman. Similarly, it would be incorrect to analyze *boy* in b as inanimate and nonhuman, while it would be correct to analyze it as animate and human. Thus, Postal's adaptation of Chomsky's lexical substitution rule not only partially defines the notion of a "violation," but also partially defines the more general notion of "possible, but incorrect, grammatical analysis." In this sense, b receives a correct grammatical analysis if its object noun is analyzed as having the features of (1-1); it receives an incorrect grammatical analysis if its object noun is analyzed as having the features of c. Thus, incorrect analyses occur when there is an incompatibility between grammatical and lexical features.

Perhaps instead of "incorrect" analyses, we should speak of "partially incorrect" analyses. After all, c does not give a completely incorrect analysis of *boy* in b. It correctly analyzes *boy* as being [+N, +SINGULAR, +CONCRETE, +PHYS. OBJ., −PRO, +COUNT]; it errs only in the animate and human features. Note that we can define the notion "degree of incorrect analysis" as the number of incompatibilities in the sentence. Now we can define the notion "partially grammatical" in terms of "partially incorrect analysis," and we can define "degree of grammaticality" in terms of "degree of incorrect analysis." We will say that a sentence, S, is fully grammatical with respect to a grammar, G, if it has at least one correct analysis with respect to G (that is, if it has at least one derivation in G with no incompatibilities). No matter how many possible incorrect analyses a sentence may have, we still will consider it fully grammatical if it has one correct analysis. We will say that a sentence is "deviant" or partially grammatical with respect to G if it has no fully correct analysis in G. Furthermore, we will define the degree of grammaticalness of a sentence as the lowest degree of incorrect analysis that it has. This is simply a restatement and an extension of long-accepted notions in transformational linguistics.

In actual performance, speakers usually attempt to give sentences the most correct analysis that they can. Speakers usually understand a sentence in terms of the best analysis that they can give it, though in certain very natural situations they can provide other, less correct, analyses. A good example of this comes about in punning. Consider the following dialogue:

"My, you look sheepish today!"
"You boar me."
"Ugh! That leaves me colt."
"Oh, stop horsing around."
"Why, am I getting your goat?"
"Oh, I can't bear any more of this!"

As is quite obvious, such puns depend upon our being able to find possible, but partially incorrect, analyses of these sentences in which the names of animals appear. Thus, *bear* in the last sentence must be analyzed as a noun meaning "a large furry animal" in order for the pun to be understood.

C MARKEDNESS

C.1 MARKEDNESS IN PHONOLOGY

Chomsky and Halle have recently revived and extended the Prague school notion of markedness for distinctive features in an attempt to account for a number of phenomena in phonology involving the "naturalness" of phonological elements. As the theory of generative phonology had previously been formulated, all phonological elements had equal status. This led to the inability of that theory to form an adequate basis for the explanation of certain facts.

1. Such a theory would give us no reason to believe that certain phonological elements would occur as systematic phonemes in almost every natural language, while others would be exceedingly rare. Yet this is the case. Voiced vowels and voiceless stops usually occur; voiceless vowels and lateral affricates very rarely occur.

2. A theory in which all combinations of distinctive features are on a par would give us no reason to guess that children would have a harder time learning some sounds than others. Yet this is the fact. Most children, for example, master liquids quite late, and before they master them they tend to substitute glides for them.

3. Neutralization of stop consonants in word-final position is a fairly widespread phenomenon. Present generative phonology would give us no reason for supposing that the voiceless stop would show up in such cases more often than the voiced stop. Yet the voiceless stop almost always shows up.

4. It is common for languages to have only two nasal consonants as systematic phonemes. An all-features-are-equal theory would give one no reason for thinking that one of the logically possible pairs would be more likely to occur. Yet *m* and *n* almost always turn up in this situation, while *n* and *ñ*, *m* and *n*, ŋ and *ñ*, and so on, almost never do.

This wide range of facts seems to correlate with the fact that certain speech sounds are inherently more difficult to produce than others: lateral fricatives and clicks are much harder to produce than voiceless stops; liquids are more difficult than glides, palatalized stops more difficult than unpalatalized ones; and so on.

Chomsky and Halle have produced the beginnings of a theory which may eventually explain such phenomena. In this theory, the phonological representation of an item in the lexicon is a distinctive feature matrix, but not with plus and minus values for the features; rather, each feature may be *marked* or *unmarked*. The unmarked form represents the "normal" state of the feature with respect to that segment; the marked form of a feature represents the "nonnormal" state. Thus, vowels will be unmarked for voicing in most languages. Since vowels in their normal state are voiced, there would be a universal rule stating that a vowel unmarked for voicing is voiced. We will adopt the following arbitrary convention for writing such rules:

$$[\text{u voice}] \rightarrow [+\text{voice}]/[\underline{\quad}, +\text{vocalic}, -\text{consonantal}] \quad \text{(C-1)}$$

In languages where there are voiceless vowels, these vowels would be marked for voicing in their lexical representation [see Remark C-1]. This marking would be interpreted as voicelessness by a universal rule such as:

$$[\text{m voice}] \rightarrow [-\text{voice}]/[\underline{\quad}, +\text{vocalic}, -\text{consonantal}] \quad \text{(C-2)}$$

In the evaluation procedure which is part of this theory Chomsky and Halle propose that *m*'s should be counted, but that *u*'s should not be counted. Thus, a grammar which has more marked features, more deviations from the "normal" state, would be valued less than a grammar that had fewer deviations from the "normal" state.

This is an interesting hypothesis, not only because it can account in some measure for facts like those mentioned above, but even more so because it is not immediately obvious that it will lead to the choice of empirically correct grammars. Consider the case of voicing in consonants. Here, what happens is just the reverse of what happens in vowels. In their normal state, consonants are voiceless. [See Remark C-2.] Thus, consonants unmarked for voice will be voiceless, while consonants marked for voice will be voiced. Thus, we might have the rules:

[u voice] → [−voice]/[___, +consonantal, −vocalic]   (C-3)
[m voice] → [+voice]/[___, +consonantal, −vocalic]   (C-4)

Since all unpredictably voiced consonants will be marked for voicing in the lexicon, each one will count one feature more in terms of the evaluation measure than will the corresponding unvoiced consonant. Thus, /d/'s will count one feature more than /t/'s. A priori, there is no reason why a theory which incorporates such an evaluation measure should be able to characterize adequate grammars. Yet, to the extent that the theory can be applied in its present tentative state, it seems to be able to do so.

Note that (C-1) through (C-4) have a great deal in common, and can be generalized in a number of ways. Though there is usually no point in generalizing rules which are part of linguistic theory, rather than any particular grammar, it may shed some light on the nature of markedness to look into the particular ways of generalizing such rules. One obvious way is the following:

$$\left.\begin{array}{l} [u\ voice] \rightarrow [\alpha\ voice] \\ [m\ voice] \rightarrow [\sim \alpha\ voice] \end{array}\right\}/[\text{___}, \alpha\ vocalic, \sim \alpha\ consonantal] \qquad (C\text{-}5)$$

This characterizes the interpretation of markings as a kind of assimilation. However, there is a nonobvious way of generalizing these rules which also has an interesting interpretation. We will assume that after all the rules for the interpretation of markings there will be two rules to interpret all markings that have not been interpreted up to that point:

The unmarked value for all features is minus.   (C-6)
The marked value for all features is plus.   (C-7)

Now we can accomplish the same work as (C-5) by the following rule which applies *before* (C-6) and (C-7):

[γ voice] → [∼ γ voice]/[___, +vocalic, −consonantal]   (C-8)
where $\gamma = $ m or u, and u $ = \sim$ m, m $= \sim$ u.

This essentially states that in vowels the polarity of markings changes for the feature "voice"—unmarked becomes marked and vice versa. Thus, a vowel unmarked for voice in the lexicon first becomes marked for voice by (C-8), and then becomes [+voice] by (C-7). Similarly, a vowel marked for voice in the lexicon first becomes unmarked by (C-8), and then becomes [−voice] by (C-6).

C.2 MARKEDNESS IN SYNTAX

The notion of markedness not only has a history in phonology, but has been discussed widely in questions of morphology and syntax as well. E. Benveniste speaks of the third person singular as being the unmarked form of the personal pronoun. [See Benveniste, 1946.] Similarly, other scholars have pointed out that the present seems to be the unmarked tense and that the historical present seems to be a syntactic neutralization between present and past in which the present—the unmarked form—always shows up. And it has often been observed that in questions such as *How big is he?* *big* is neutral. Thus, if we assume that *big* differs from *small* in a feature which we will call "positive degree," *big* having the value plus, *small* having the value minus, and if we furthermore assume that plus is the unmarked value for that feature, then the use of *big* in questions can also be looked upon as a case of syntactic neutralization in which the unmarked form shows up.

Thus, it seems that the notion of markedness should play a significant role in syntax as well as in phonology. Although no theory has yet been devised which will account for the above phenomena in terms of some formal notion of markedness, some progress has been made toward incorporating the notion of markedness into present syntactic theory.

Postal has observed [M.I.T. course 23.752, 1965] that certain phenomena involving number and countability in English nouns can be handled in terms of markedness as Halle has defined it. Consider the words *boy, chalk, pants,* and *people.*

a. one boy	j. *two pants	(C-9)
b. two boys	k. *a lot of pant	
c. *a lot of boy	l. a lot of pants	
d. a lot of boys	m. *one people (meaning	
e. *one chalk	"person")	
f. *two chalks	n. two people	
g. a lot of chalk	o. *a lot of people (singu-	
h. *a lot of chalks	lar)	
i. *one pant	p. a lot of people (plural)	

Boy may be either singular or plural. If it is singular, it is countable; if plural, it is either countable or uncountable. *Chalk* can be only uncountable and singular. *Pants* can be only uncountable and plural. *People* may be only plural, but may be countable or uncountable. Of these, *pants* is the least normal (most irregular), *boy* the most normal (least irregular), and *chalk* and *people* somewhere in between.

Note that a lexical representation of these items in terms of pluses and minuses fails for these items in two ways. (1) We would have to represent *pants* as being [—SINGULAR, —COUNT-ABLE]. However, there seems to be a general rule of English (and, perhaps, a universal rule of some sort) that uncountable nouns are singular. In English, as in most other languages, there are a handful of exceptions to this rule, for example, *pants, scissors, binoculars, spectacles,* and so on. In a plus-minus system, these exceptions would represent counterexamples, and cause the abandonment of the rule. In a marked-unmarked system, the rule could be stated as referring to normal (nonexceptional) nouns. The rule would be: Nouns unmarked for SINGULAR become +SINGULAR if they are —COUNTABLE. [See Rule c of (C-11).] (2) In a plus-minus system we could not represent the fact that *pants* is more irregular than *chalk. Chalk* would have to be represented [+SINGULAR, —COUNTABLE], since the value of the SINGULAR feature could not be predicted from the value of the COUNTABLE feature once the rule of (1) above was abandoned. Thus, both items would have to be represented with unpredictable values for both features.

Postal has noted that both of these failures can be remedied with the lexical representation of (C-10) and the rules of (C-11). Note that an evaluation measure would count m's, but not u's.

	boy	chalk	pants	people	(C-10)
SINGULAR	u	u	m	m	
COUNTABLE	u	m	m	u	

Thus, *pants* with two marked values is most deviant, *people* and *chalk* with one m are next, and *boy* with none is completely regular with respect to these features. To account for the facts in (C-9), Postal has proposed rules like the following for the interpretation of markings:

(C-11)

a. [m SINGULAR] → [—SINGULAR]

b. [m COUNTABLE] → [—COUNTABLE]

c. [u SINGULAR] → [+SINGULAR]/[__, —COUNTABLE]

d. [u SINGULAR] → $\begin{Bmatrix} [+SINGULAR] \\ [-SINGULAR] \end{Bmatrix}$

e. [u COUNTABLE] → [+COUNTABLE]/
   [__, +SINGULAR]

f. [u COUNTABLE] → $\begin{Bmatrix} [-COUNTABLE] \\ [+COUNTABLE] \end{Bmatrix}$

Note that ordering is crucial in these rules. There are two sources for the feature [—COUNTABLE], Rules b and f. Rule c operates in the environment [—COUNTABLE] which is supplied by Rule b, not that supplied by Rule f. Ordering in this case allows us to refer to the uncountable nouns which were originally marked (the products of Rule b). Rule c handles ordinary mass nouns like *chalk*, which must be marked in the lexicon for countability since that uncountability is not predictable. Rule c says, essentially, that mass nouns are predictably singular. Plurals may function like uncountable nouns. As Rule f states, the normal state for plural nouns may be either countable or uncountable (for example, *a lot of boys* or *two boys*). Note that plural nouns have two sources, Rules a and d. *People* is a product of Rule a; boys is a product of Rule d. Both are subject to Rule e, which accounts for items b, d, n, and p of (C-9).

The notion of markedness can shed light on a number of other previously unexplained problems in syntax. Consider, for example, the case of stative and nonstative adjectives and verbs.

It has long been observed that adjectives normally indicate states, properties, or conditions, while verbs usually indicate activity. That is, it is normal for an adjective to be stative, while it is normal for a verb to be nonstative. However, there are exceptions, and in previous work in formal linguistics the exceptions forced us to abandon the rule. Given a theory like that presented in Chomsky's *Aspects*, the fact that there exist stative verbs and nonstative adjectives in fairly random distribution in English would force us to conclude that the features STATIVE and ADJECTIVAL were cross-classified and that one could not, for the great majority of cases, predict the value of one feature from that of the other. In such a theory, the verbs *hit, know, noisy,* and *tall* would be represented in the lexicon in the following way:

	hit	*know*	*noisy*	*tall*	(C-12)
STATIVE	—	+	—	+	
ADJECTIVAL	—	—	+	+	

Since only nonstative verbs can form imperatives and progressives, we get a of (C-13), but not b of (C-13).

a. Don't hit him!   (C-13)
   Don't be noisy!
   They are hitting him.
   They are being noisy.
b. *Don't know that fact!
   *Don't be tall!
   *They are knowing that fact.
   *They are being tall.

Given the concept of markedness, we can easily state the generalization that adjectives are normally stative and verbs normally nonstative. [See Remark C-3.] Where there are exceptions, we can mark them in the lexicon. Suppose that we know the value of the feature STATIVE in terms of pluses and minuses for each lexical item. We can then mark the abnormal cases, the stative verbs and nonstative adjectives, with the feature [m ADJECTIVAL], and leave the normal cases unmarked.

	hit	*know*	*noisy*	*tall*	(C-14)
ADJECTIVAL	u	m	m	u	

The following rules will interpret these markings correctly:

(C-15)

a. [u ADJECTIVAL] → [−ADJECTIVAL]/
   [__, −STATIVE]

b. [u ADJECTIVAL] → [+ADJECTIVAL]/
   [__, +STATIVE]

c. [m ADJECTIVAL] → [+ADJECTIVAL]/
   [__, −STATIVE]

d. [m ADJECTIVAL] → [−ADJECTIVAL]/
   [__, +STATIVE]

It is interesting that these rules are almost identical in form to rules (C-1), (C-2), (C-3), and (C-4), respectively, which interpreted the markings for voicedness in vowels and consonants. Like those rules, (C-15) is subject to generalization of the same sort:

(C-16)

$$\left. \begin{array}{l} [\text{u ADJECTIVAL}] \rightarrow [\alpha \text{ ADJECTIVAL}] \\ [\text{m ADJECTIVAL}] \rightarrow [\sim \alpha \text{ ADJECTIVAL}] \end{array} \right\} /$$
$$[\text{\_\_}, \alpha \text{ STATIVE}]$$

or

(C-17)

$$[\gamma \text{ ADJECTIVAL}] \rightarrow [\sim \gamma \text{ ADJECTIVAL}]/$$
$$[\text{\_\_}, -\text{STATIVE}]$$

assuming that all *m*'s will later be interpreted as pluses and all *u*'s as minuses.

Thus, our use of the concept of markedness reveals that this case in syntax is exactly parallel to a case in phonology.

D CONTEXTUAL FEATURES

Chomsky [1965b] discussed two positions on contextual features. (1) Selectional restriction features (for example, on verbs) refer to individual features in preceding or following items (for example, nouns). For instance, a verb that takes animate subjects and abstract objects would be represented with a conjunction of two selectional features:

$$[+ [+ANIMATE]\_\_] \text{ and } [+\_\_[+ABSTRACT]] \quad (D\text{-}1)$$

each referring to individual features in surrounding items. (2) Selectional restrictions are single unanalyzable features. The facts represented by the two features of (D-1) would instead be represented by a single, entirely different feature:

$$[+ [+ANIMATE]\_\_[+ABSTRACT]] \qquad (D\text{-}2)$$

Though, in notation, (D-1) and (D-2) look similar, they would be interpreted as totally different. (D-2), as an unanalyzable unit, could share nothing with either feature of (D-1).

Chomsky eventually chose the representation of (D-2) [for discussion, see Section E.1 below]. This position seems untenable to me for two reasons:

a. Many verbs have partially similar properties; they can take the same subject, while taking different objects—and vice versa. Representing selectional restrictions as unanalyzable features does not allow for the description of these similarities.

b. There are a number of rules involving selectional restric-

144

tions that cannot be stated in terms of unanalyzable contextual features.

D.1 LEXICAL SIMILARITIES

Consider the words *run* and *throw*. Both must take animate subjects, and any native speaker of English knows that they have this property in common. However, *throw* is transitive and takes a physical object, while *run* is intransitive (in the sense of *John ran across the street*). If we consider contextual features as unanalyzable, these words will have the following feature specifications:

run: [+ [+ANIMATE]__]   (D-3)
throw: [+ [+ANIMATE]__[+PHYS. OBJ.]]

That is, *run* and *throw* will not be represented as though they had anything in common. For this reason, unanalyzable contextual features fail to describe a significant part of our linguistic knowledge.

D.2 REGULARITIES INVOLVING CONTEXTUAL FEATURES

D.21 Subjects of Transitive Verbs

Barbara Hall [1965] has observed that in an overwhelming number of cases, the subject of a transitive verb is animate. As she pointed out, there are many apparent exceptions to this rule which are indeed only apparent. For example, in

John broke the window with the bat.   (D-4)
The bat broke the window.   (D-5)

the logical relation of *bat* to *break* seems to be the same—that of an instrumental. Dr. Hall suggests that *bat* is an instrumental in the deep structure of both sentences, and that (D-5) is really subjectless or has some sort of indefinite subject. Thus, (D-5) would be derived from

Broke the window with the bat.   (D-6)

This analysis, besides accounting for the instrumental sense of *bat* in (D-5), would allow us to maintain the above rule by claiming that when *break* takes a subject, it must be an animate one.

In Appendix A, we saw that, on independent grounds, we had to hypothesize that verbs like *surprise, amuse,* and so on, that appeared to take abstract subjects and animate objects really took animate subjects and abstract objects in the deep structure. Thus, we removed another class of apparent exceptions. However, there are some real exceptions to Dr. Hall's generalization. Verbs like

> *precede, follow, imply, mean, indicate, entail* (D-7)

may take both abstract subjects and abstract objects.

I suggest that these exceptions not be viewed as counterexamples to the generalization; instead, I would view the generalization as a statement about the normal or unmarked form of subject of transitive verbs. If we assume the notion of markedness *and* if we assume that contextual features are not unanalyzable, we can state the rule easily:

$$[\text{u ANIMATE\_\_}] \rightarrow [+\text{ANIMATE\_\_}]/[+\_\_\text{NP}, \_\_]\quad\text{(D-8)}$$

By (C-7) above, [m ANIMATE__] will become [−ANIMATE__]. Thus, verbs like those in (D-7) can be viewed quite reasonably as being nonnormal cases that contain the feature [m ANIMATE__].

D.22 Objects of Stative Transitive Verbs

It is normally the case that a stative transitive verb with an animate subject *may* take a non-PHYSICAL OBJECT object.

Examples: (D-9)
a. verbs: *see, hear, feel, know, believe, consider, bother, amuse, surprise, amaze*
b. adjectives: *good for, eager for, anxious about, fond of*
Exceptions:
angry at, fearful of, sympathetic toward, respect, admire

A rule to state this might look like:

(D-10)

$$[\text{u \_\_PHYS. OBJ. (L)}] \rightarrow [\alpha \text{\_\_PHYS. OBJ. (L)}]/$$

$$\begin{bmatrix} \alpha \text{ PHYS. OBJ. (G)} \\ +\text{NP (G)} \\ +\text{STATIVE}\quad\text{(G)} \end{bmatrix}$$

D.23 Abstract Subjects and Objects

Given these rules, a rule can be stated about a subclass of the exceptions to the rule of (D-8). Verbs that take inanimate subjects and non-PHYSICAL OBJECT objects must take non-PHYSICAL OBJECT subjects.

$$(D-11)$$

$$[u \text{ PHYS. OBJ. } \_\_(L)] \rightarrow [\_\_ \text{ PHYS. OBJ. } \_\_(L)]/$$

$$\begin{bmatrix} -\text{ANIMATE}\_\_(G) \\ -\_\_\text{PHYS. OBJ. (G)} \end{bmatrix}$$

Examples are:

precede, follow, imply, mean, indicate, entail (D-12)

These are just the verbs mentioned in (D-7) above which are exceptions to (D-8). However, there may be other exceptions to (D-8) that do not fall within the domain of (D-11), namely, any stative verb exceptions to (D-8).

E ON THE FORM OF LEXICAL ITEMS

E.1 UNANALYZABLE CONTEXTUAL FEATURES

Chomsky's reason for adopting the position that features are un-analyzable was the fact that in some cases there is a dependency between the contextual features involving the subject and those involving the object. The example he cites is the following [Chomsky, 1965b, p. 119]:

a. He _____ the platoon.   (E-1)
b. His decision to resign _____ the platoon.
c. His decision to resign _____ our respect.

Chomsky points out that *command* may occur in a and c, but not in b, while *baffle* may occur in a and b, but not in c. He concludes that if we allow contextual features to refer separately to subjects and to objects, then we would have to specify *command* as having the features:

(E-2)

[[+ANIMATE] Aux__], [__Det [+ANIMATE]],
[[+ABSTRACT] Aux__], and __Det [+ABSTRACT]]

However, such a specification would not show the dependency between subject and object, illustrated by the inability of *command* to occur in b. On these grounds Chomsky concludes that the proper way to express such a dependency is to require each contextual feature to refer both to the subject and to the object restrictions. He would have the lexical entry for *command* contain the unanalyzable features:

148

(E-3)

[[+ANIMATE] Aux__Det [+ANIMATE]] and
[[+ABSTRACT] Aux__Det [+ABSTRACT]]

However, there is another way to express dependencies between subject and object without requiring unanalyzable features, namely, to allow lexical entries to be Boolean functions of features. Using such a formalism we can represent the contextual restrictions on *command* in the following way:

(E-4)

((([[+ANIMATE] Aux__] and [__Det [+ANIMATE]] ∨
[[+ABSTRACT] Aux__] and [__Det [+ABSTRACT]]))

The use of disjunctions in lexical representation is by no means new. Fodor and Katz's lexical items employ Boolean functions of semantic markers. [See Fodor and Katz, 1964a.] In fact, since the lexical meaning of *command* differs in a and c of (E-1), a lexical representation for *command* which took account of semantic markers as well as syntactic features would be phrased essentially in Fodor-Katz form, and the question of disjunctions among purely syntactic features would never arise in the case of *command*. [See Remark E-1.] However, the point in question is relevant in other cases. Consider

a. John prevented Bill from assassinating Bundy. (E-5)
b. John prevented Bill's assassination of Bundy.

Some transformational linguists would analyze these sentences as having rather different underlying structures, while assigning *prevent* the same lexical meaning in both cases. In this case, the problem of the dependency between object and complement arises —assuming that this analysis and others of the same sort are correct. I propose that we handle all such cases by allowing lexical items to be represented as Boolean functions of features.

E.2 DEFINITION OF MULTIPLE ANALYSIS

When a lexical item has a disjunction of syntactic features associated with a single lexical meaning, we will say that that lexical item has a "multiple analysis" with respect to that meaning. When a lexical item has only a simple conjunction of syntactic features (with negation allowed only over individual features) associated with a lexical item, we will say that the lexical item has a "single analysis" with respect to that meaning.

E.3 CONJUNCTION OF CONTEXTUAL FEATURES

Note that we can interpret Chomsky's notion of a conjunction of contextual features as being rather different than his notion of a conjunction of inherent features. For example, Chomsky [1965b, p. 85] presents as a sample lexical representation for *sincerity*: [+N, −COUNT, +ABSTRACT]. Such a lexical item could be inserted only into a complex symbol that had *all* of the features +N *and* −COUNT *and* +ABSTRACT. However, a conjunction of contextual features is interpreted rather differently. On page 94 of the same work, Chomsky gives as a sample lexical representation for *grow*: [+V, +__NP, +__#, +__ADJECTIVE]. This does not mean that *grow* can be inserted only into a complex symbol containing all of the features +V *and* +__NP *and* +__# *and* +__ADJECTIVE. Obviously, such a complex symbol does not exist. Rather, the representation for *grow* means that *grow* may be inserted into a complex symbol that has the feature +V and has *either* +__NP *or* +__# *or* +__ADJECTIVE. Under this interpretation, conjunctions of contextual features represent disjunctions each of which may be conjoined to inherent features. However, conjunctions of inherent features remain conjunctions under this interpretation.

E.4 BOOLEAN FUNCTIONS OF FEATURES

Boolean functions seem to be necessary not only for contextual features, but for other types of syntactic features as well. A clear case of this can be found in Latin (as well as in other case languages) in kinds of irregular forms called "heteroclites." Bennett [1960, p. 32] lists the following as an example of this phenomenon:

> Several nouns have the entire singular of one declension, while the plural is of another; as,
>
> vās, vāsis (vessel);   Plu., vāsa, vāsōrum, vāsīs,   (E-6)
>   etc.
> jūgerum, jūgerī (acre); Plu., jūgera, jūgerum,
>   jūgeribus, etc.

If we do not allow Boolean functions of syntactic features, it is not at all clear that one can state facts like this in lexical items as they are presently conceived. One could, of course, write *ad hoc* rules for each such case, for instance,

$$[3 \text{ Declension}] \rightarrow [2 \text{ Declension}] / \begin{bmatrix} \overline{} \\ -\text{Singular} \\ vas \end{bmatrix} \qquad (E\text{-}7)$$

Such a solution is unsatisfying for two reasons: (1) Declension does not seem to be a feature that can change in a transformational rule, and it is only in cases like this that one would need to change the declension of a noun. (2) This is a fact about an individual lexical item, not a regularity of the grammar, and therefore, should be represented in the lexicon.

With Boolean functions of syntactic features, such facts can easily be represented in the lexicon. We would associate with *vas* the entry

> *vas* ((3 Declension and +Singular) ∨ (2 Declension   (E-8)
> and −Singular))

Suppose such a lexical entry were inserted into the lexical member of a complex symbol with the following grammatical features:

Noun

$$
\left[
\begin{array}{l}
+N \\
3 \text{ Declension} \\
-\text{Singular} \quad ,
\end{array}
\right]
\qquad\qquad \text{(E-9)}
$$

We assume that [3 Declension] and [2 Declension] belong to an antonymous set (there is, their conjunction is a contradiction). Note that each branch of the disjunction of (E-8) is incompatible with the grammatical member of (E-9). When this is the case, we will say that we have a violation. This is a natural extension of the notion of a violation introduced in Section 1.51. Similarly, we can extend our interpretation of this system in terms of the sentential calculus [see Section 1.52] in an obvious way so that such a notion of a violation is equivalent to the logical notion of a contradition. In (E-10),

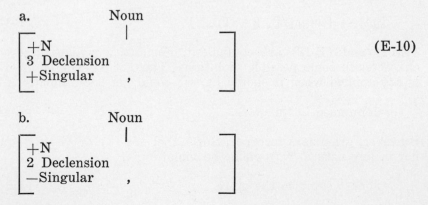

a.   Noun

$$
\left[
\begin{array}{l}
+N \\
3 \text{ Declension} \\
+\text{Singular} \quad ,
\end{array}
\right]
\qquad\qquad \text{(E-10)}
$$

b.   Noun

$$
\left[
\begin{array}{l}
+N \\
2 \text{ Declension} \\
-\text{Singular} \quad ,
\end{array}
\right]
$$

the grammatical member of both a and b is compatible with one branch of (E-8). In these cases there is no violation, as is consistent with our sentential calculus analogy.

Note that we now can think of the Boolean function of features that comprises a lexical item as stating a set of conditions that the grammatical member of the complex symbol must meet. Note also that the grammatical member is *not* a Boolean function, but simply a conjunction of features.

One question that might be raised is: How will rules apply to complex symbols containing Boolean functions? That is, suppose we have a rule that applies only to a [+Singular] segment, would it apply to a complex symbol whose lexical member had [+Singular] in one branch of a disjunction and [−Singular] in the other? The answer, of course, is that the rule will not even look at the lexical member, but will operate only on the grammatical member. Since the grammatical member is a simple conjunction, this question will simply never arise.

E.5 SUPPLETION

Suppletion is a common phenomenon and occurs in most languages. A widely discussed example of it in English is the alternation between *go* and *went*. Chomsky [1957] suggested that suppletion be handled by rules, for example,

$$go + \text{PAST} \to went \tag{E-11}$$

The addition of syntactic features to the theoretical apparatus of transformational theory does not change this very much. Instead of (E-11) we might have:

$$[+\text{PAST}, go] \to [went] \tag{E-12}$$

or

$$[go] \to [went]/[+\text{PAST}, \_\_] \tag{E-13}$$

(E-11) and (E-12) are equivalent. Formulations like these can characterize some possible violations. Thus, if (E-11) or (E-12) is not applied when it should be, we could get such violations as

$$\text{*John goed to the store.} \tag{E-14}$$

However, grammars incorporating either (E-11) or (E-12) could not in any natural way yield the violation.

$$\text{*John wented to the store.} \tag{E-15}$$

A grammar incorporating (E-13) could generate (E-15), provided that *went* were introduced with a marker indicating that it normally could not undergo the rule that places *-ed* on past tense verbs. However, no English grammar in present linguistic theory that introduces *went* only by rules such as (E-11), (E-12), or (E-13) can naturally characterize the very common violation:

*John has went to the store.   (E-16)

(E-16) is understood as being an incorrect form of

John has gone to the store.   (E-17)

and a descriptively adequate grammar of English should provide that information.

Moreover, violations such as (E-16) seem to reflect not a misapplication of a rule, but rather an incorrect lexical selection. This would indicate that perhaps suppletion should be represented in the lexicon rather than by rule. This makes good sense, since suppletion always represents facts about individual lexical items, rather than generalizations about the language. If suppletion is to be represented in the lexicon, we will have to extend further our notion of what a lexical item is. So far, we have characterized a lexical item as having a single phonological matrix conjoined with a Boolean function of syntactic and semantic features. We can handle suppletion by allowing the phonological matrices to enter into Boolean functions with syntactic features. Thus, a (very simplified) version of the entry for *go-went* might be:

                                                                (E-18)
[[*go* and +PRESENT] or [*went* and −PRESENT]]
and [all other features]

However, such a representation presents difficulties that a Boolean function of syntactic features does not present. If we assume, as is done at present, that phonological rules operate on the phonological features in the lexical member of the complex symbol, then we cannot simply insert an entire lexical item such as (E-18) into the lexical member, since it would not be clear whether the phonological rules should operate on *go* or *went*. If we want to maintain the assumption that phonological rules operate on the phonological features of the lexical member, then we would have to find an appropriate way of choosing one phonological matrix. We can do this quite easily. We incorporate into linguistic theory a mechanical procedure which converts each lexical item into some disjunctive normal form with respect to phonological matrices, that is, a disjunction, each member of which contains

only one phonological matrix. For example, such a normal form
for (E-18) would be:

(E-19)

[[*go* and +PRESENT and all other features] or
[*went* and —PRESENT and all other features]]

We would then revise our lexical selection rule to choose at random
one branch of a lexical item's disjunction of features. Then, if the
branch containing *went* were chosen, and if it were incompatible
with the grammatical member of the complex symbol, we would
get a violation. If it were compatible, we would get no violation.
The same would be true if we choose the branch containing *go*.

Of course, we need not assume that the phonological rules
apply to the phonological features of the lexical member. We might
instead assume the following: Let the base component randomly
generate a phonological matrix as part of the grammatical member of the complex symbol. Let a lexical item of the form of (E-18)
be inserted in the lexical member, and check to see if the phonological matrix of the grammatical member is compatible with *any*
phonological matrix in the lexical member. If not, we get a violation.
If so, we then apply the phonological rules to the features of the
grammatical member of the complex symbol. With such conventions, we can extend our interpretation of the lexical member as
a set of conditions that the grammatical member must meet.

The latter solution has certain advantages. One of the difficulties that Halle has experienced in utilizing his notion of markedness is that, although he can now easily express certain universal
constraints on morphemes [such as (C-5)], his system can no
longer easily express the morpheme structure rules of a *particular*
language. That is, his system in its present incompletely formulated
state, cannot capture the notion of a well-formed morpheme of
English. Now we can add this notion in a fairly simple way.

Let the base generate a random matrix of phono-   (E-20)
logical features as part of the grammatical member
of the complex symbol. These features will contain
values of + and —. Apply the morpheme structure
rules of English to this matrix, interpreting the rules
not as filling in blanks, but as substituting features
under identity. That is, the rule will *be applicable* if
the randomly generated matrix meets the structural
description of the rule. It will *apply* only if the features to be inserted by the rule are identical to the
corresponding features of the randomly generated
matrix. If this is not so, we will say the rule is
violated, and the randomly generated matrix is not
a well-formed morpheme of English. The mor-

pheme structure rules will apply before lexical insertion. Now insert a lexical item as the lexical member of the complex symbol. Its features will have values in u and m not in $+$ and $-$. Now apply the universal rules to convert the u's and m's into $+$'s and $-$'s. Then check to see if the grammatical matrix is compatible with any phonological matrix in the lexical member.

F PASSIVES, ADVERBS, AND QUANTIFIERS

F.1 PASSIVES AND MANNER ADVERBIALS

In Chapter 2, we claimed that verbs like *owe, resemble, weigh,* and so on were exceptions to the passive transformation. It is not obvious that this is so. Chomsky [1965b, p. 104] makes the opposite claim. He proposes that the fact that such verbs do not undergo the passive transformation can be predicted from the fact that they do not take manner adverbials freely. He proposes to describe this by introducing a PASSIVE morpheme as an optional constituent of the node MANNER. Thus, he would have the rule: MANNER → by PASSIVE. The passive transformation would be obligatorily triggered by the PASSIVE morpheme. It would follow, then, that only verbs which could take manner adverbs freely (that is, could occur in the same simplex S as the constituent manner), could undergo the passive transformation. Those verbs which could not take manner adverbials freely (that is, could not co-occur with the constituent MANNER) could not conceivably undergo the passive, since they could never occur in a simple sentence in which the morpheme PASSIVE was introduced.

Chomsky's analysis does not account for such verbs as *know, believe, consider, think, see, hear, perceive,* and so on. These verbs, like other stative verbs, may not take manner adverbials freely, but may undergo the passive transformation. Consider the following sentences:

a. Everyone knew that Bill was tall.   (F-1)
    *Everyone knew cleverly that Bill was tall.
    That Bill was tall was know by everyone.
b. Bill believed that Harry was president.

*Bill believed cleverly that Harry was president.
It was believed by Bill that Harry was president.
c. John considered Harry a fink.
*John considered Harry a fink with great en-
thusiasm.
Harry was considered a fink by John.
d. John thought that Harry deserted Jill.
*John thought masterfully that Harry deserted
Jill.
It was thought by John that Harry deserted Jill.
e. John saw Harry.
*John saw Harry industriously.
Harry was seen by John.
f. John heard the music.
*John heard the music carefully.
The music was heard by John.

If we were to maintain Chomsky's analysis and extend our grammar of English to account for these cases, we would have to introduce the PASSIVE morpheme in some other constituent as well as in MANNER. This would mean introducing the PASSIVE morpheme twice in different parts of the phrase structure. Such a solution would lack generality. Moreover, it would fail to predict the fact that *resemble, owe, have,* and so on do not undergo the passive. Note that all these verbs are stative, as are those of (F-1). To permit the verbs of (F-1) to undergo the PASSIVE transformation, we would have to introduce our second occurrence of the PASSIVE morpheme so that it, unlike manner, could freely co-occur with stative verbs. To avoid the passivization of *resemble, owe,* and so on, we would have to indicate in the lexicon that these verbs could not occur with the PASSIVE morpheme. Thus, these verbs are exceptional, even considering Chomsky's analysis of the passive construction.

F.2 THE SOURCE OF SOME MANNER ADVERBIALS

It seems possible to predict the occurrences of many manner adverbials from occurrences of another, more basic construction. Many manner adverbials correspond exactly to adjectives that take predicate complements. For example,

A. 1. a. John hangs from trees. (F-2)
   b. John hangs from trees recklessly.
   c. John is reckless in hanging from trees.
   2. a. Moss hangs from trees.
   b. *Moss hangs from trees recklessly.
   c. *Moss is reckless in hanging from trees.

    3. a. John was tall.
       b. *John was tall recklessly.
       c. *John was reckless in being tall.
B. 1. a. The tailor fitted me.
       b. The tailor fitted me carefully.
       c. The tailor was careful in fitting me.
   2. a. The suit fit me.
       b. *The suit fit me carefully.
       c. *The suit was careful in fitting me.
   3. a. The tailor knew about suits.
       b. *The tailor knew about suits carefully.
       c. *The tailor was careful in knowing about suits.
C. 1. a. John sharpened knives.
       b. John sharpened knives cautiously.
       c. John was cautious in sharpening knives.
   2. a. The machine sharpened knives.
       b. *The machine sharpened knives cautiously.
       c. *The machine was cautious in sharpening knives.
   3. a. John resembled his mother.
       b. *John resembled his mother cautiously.
       c. *John was cautious in resembling his mother.

As these sentences illustrate, the adjectives in the c sentences share co-occurrence restrictions with the adverbs in the b sentences. Note that all the adjectives in the c sentences are restricted in that the complement that follows them may not have a verb (or adjective) that is stative, as is illustrated by the 3 sentences. Note also that each of the adjectives in the c sentences must meet the SD of ID-NP-DEL.

If we derive the b sentences from c sentences, not only can we account for the relationship between them, but we also can simplify the grammar of English in a number of ways. First, we can eliminate the constituent MANNER from the phrase structure. Secondly, we can account for the co-occurrence restrictions between subjects and manner adverbs without any new selectional apparatus. These restrictions will follow from the selectional restrictions between subjects and adjectives. Thus, the fact that we do not get *The suit fit me carefully* will follow from the fact that we do not get *The suit was careful in fitting me*. Thirdly, we will be able to account for the fact that many adjective complements may not contain manner adverbials. Consider the following sentences:

A. 1. a. John was careful at playing gin rummy.   (F-3)
       b. *John was careful at playing gin rummy well.

c. *John was careful at being good at playing gin rummy.
d. John was good at playing gin rummy.
e. John played gin rummy well.
2. a. John was clever at making decisions.
   b. *John was clever at making decisions wisely.
   c. *John was clever at being wise at making decisions.
   d. John was wise at making decisions.
   e. John made decisions wisely.

The nonoccurrence of the b sentences follows from the nonoccurrence of the c sentences. The c sentences do not occur since the matrix adjectives (that is, *careful, clever*) may not take stative verbs or adjectives in their complements (that is, *good, wise*). However, there do exist cases in which manner adverbs may occur in adjective complements.

B. 1. a. John was good at playing gin rummy carefully.   (F-3)
      b. John was good at being careful at playing gin rummy.
   2. a. John was wise in making decisions cautiously.
      b. John was wise in being cautious at making decisions.

The grammaticalness of a follows from the grammaticalness of b in each example. The b sentences are grammatical since *good* and *wise* must take nonstative verbs or adjectives in their complements. *Careful* and *cautious* are nonstative, as can be seen by the fact that they occur in imperative, progressive, and do-something constructions. For example,

1. a. Be careful.   (F-4)
   b. Be cautious.
2. a. We are being careful.
   b. We are being cautious.
3. a. What we are doing is being careful.
   b. What we are doing is being cautious.

F.3 PSEUDO-PASSIVES

Suppose we adopt our proposed derivation of manner adverbs and thereby do away with the constituent MANNER of the verb phrase. Chomsky's analysis in which the PASSIVE morpheme is a constituent of MANNER will then have to be abandoned.

Since that analysis is inadequate anyway, as we have seen, our proposal should not hurt our ability to describe the normal passive construction. However, one of Chomsky's major reasons for adopting his analysis of the passive is that it supposedly accounts for the pseudo-passive construction as well as for the normal passive. We can maintain Chomsky's analysis of the pseudo-passive by allowing an optional PASSIVE constituent to be introduced in the verb phrase in the same position where MANNER had previously been introduced. However, it seems that Chomsky's analysis of pseudo-passive is also open to question—no matter how we analyze manner adverbials.

Among the pseudo-passives that Chomsky attempts to account for are:

    a. The proposal was vehemently argued against.   (F-5)
    b. The new course of action was agreed on.
    c. John is looked up to by everyone.
    d. This job is being worked at quite seriously.
    e. The boat was decided on by John.

Chomsky assumes that these sentences have deep structures containing intransitive verbs followed by prepositional phrases within the verb phrase. For example:

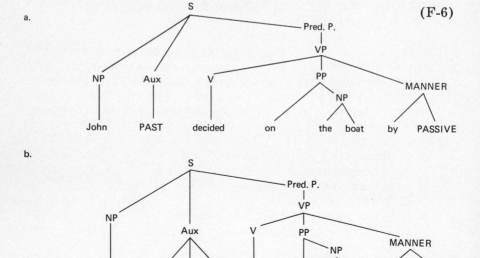

He then postulates that the passive transformation has the following structural description:

NP-Aux-V- . . . -NP- . . . -by passive. . . .   (F-7)
(where the leftmost . . . does not contain an NP)

(F-6) will meet this structural description, Chomsky argues, even though it contains an intransitive verb. This will account for the pseudo-passives of Sentences d and e of (F-5). Pseudo-passives, in general, Chomsky claims, come from prepositional phrases dominated by VP, following intransitive verbs, and preceding the constituent MANNER (and, hence, the PASSIVE morpheme). Under these general conditions, the structural description of (H) will be met.

Such an analysis, Chomsky maintains, will also account for the nonoccurrence of certain pseudo-passives. For example, *Someone is working at the office* does not passivize to become *The office is being worked at*. Moreover, *John decided on the boat* is ambiguous and means either (a) *John chose the boat* or (b) *John decided while he was on the boat*. With the meaning (a), it has the structure of a in (F-6) and passivizes to become e of (F-5). But e of (F-5) is not ambiguous—it corresponds only to the meaning of (a), not to that of (b). Chomsky accounts for this by hypothesizing that the following structure corresponds to the (b) meaning:

(F-8)

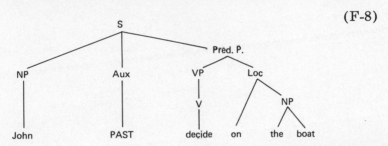

Note that *on the boat* in (F-8) is a locative phrase which is *not* a constituent of VP. It, therefore, could never occur to the left of MANNER (and hence, PASSIVE) and so could never meet the structural description of the passive as given in (F-8). The same is true for *Someone is working at the office*.

(F-9)

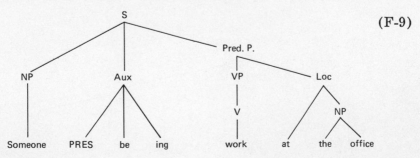

This analysis depends strongly on the existence of a PASSIVE morpheme introduced within the VP constituent and at the end of it. We will try to show that the facts accounted for by this analysis also can be accounted for by an analysis that does not make this assumption. Then we will attempt to show that Chomsky's analysis is inadequate in that it predicts the existence of pseudo-passives that do not, in fact, exist.

Chomsky views *work* and *decide* as intransitive verbs that may optionally be followed by a prepositional phrase. If we assume that all verbs are followed by prepositions at some point in their derivations [see A.1 in Appendix A], then *work* and *decide* can be looked on as transitive verbs that do not undergo the rule that deletes prepositions that follow verbs. Under this analysis we can consider *They decided on the boat* and *They chose the boat* to have the same deep structures. In Chomsky's analysis their structures are entirely different.

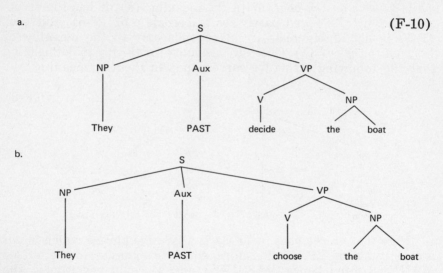

a.   (F-10)

b.

After preposition-spelling we would have:

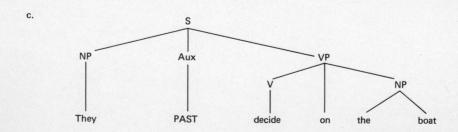

c.

d.

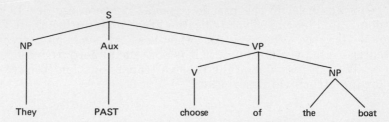

Note that *decide* is irregular in taking the preposition *on*. This irregularity would have to be handled in either Chomsky's analysis or in ours. If nominalization occurred at this point we would get *their choice* of *the boat*. Preposition deletion later applies to *choose* but not to *decide*, yielding *They decided on the boat* and *They chose the boat*.

Sentences like

| They decided. | (F-11) |
| They worked. | (F-12) |

can now be looked at as reduced forms of

| They decided on something. | (F-13) |
| They worked at something. | (F-14) |

Decide on and *work at* would then be considered as verbs like *eat* which allow unspecified objects to be deleted. Thus, *John worked at the office* and *John decided on the boat* (meaning "while he was on the boat") might have the structures (after preposition spelling):

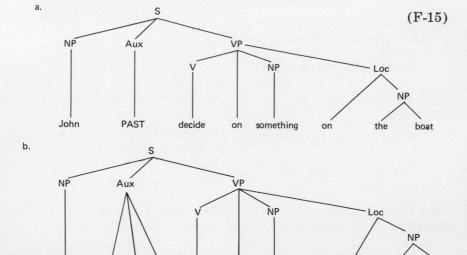

a.   (F-15)

(Our analysis of the pseudo-passive does not require LOC to be dominated by a special predicate phrase node rather than VP. That node may be necessary for other reasons, such as correctly sub-categorizing verbs, but since it is not crucial here we omit it.)

We can now define the passive transformation to have the following structural description:

(F-16)

NP-AUX-V- . . . NP- . . .
(where the leftmost . . . does not contain an NP and where the rightmost NP is directly dominated by VP)

We could then allow the passive to be an optional rule, or we could have it triggered by some passive marker, which might, for example, be a feature of the verb, but which need not be a constituent of MANNER or VP. If we assume that the rule that deletes an unspecified object comes *after* our passive transformation, we can account for all the facts that Chomsky accounts for. Suppose the passive is an optional rule. If it applies to (F-15) we will get *something was decided on on the boat* and *something is being worked at at the office*. If the passive does not apply, then the object deletion rule can apply to yield *John decided on the boat* and *John is working at the office*.

Chomsky's analysis of the passive yields some incorrect results that our analysis does not yield. In stating his "strictly local sub-categorization" principle, [1965, pp. 102–103], Chomsky points out that prepositional phrases of direction and place must be introduced as constituents of VP since they determine the strict sub-categorization of verbs. For example,

dash—into the room (V—Direction)   (F-17)
remain—in England (V—Place)
*dash—in England
*remain—into the room

Note that *dash* and *remain* both take manner adverbials. For example,

1. John dashed into the room $\begin{cases}\text{impatiently.} \\ \text{with great enthusiasm.}\end{cases}$ (F-18)

2. John remained in England $\begin{cases}\text{patiently.} \\ \text{with some regret.}\end{cases}$

Each of these sentences could, therefore, meet Chomsky's proposed structural description for the passive (H), and we would get:

1. *The room was dashed into by John.   (F-19)

2. *England was remained in by John.

Note that since the SD of our passive transformation required that VP directly dominate the object NP, these nonsentences will not be generated under our analysis.

F.4 FURTHER REMARKS ON MANNER ADVERBIALS

We are now prepared to offer further evidence that many manner adverbials are derived from adjectival complements. Consider the following sentences:

    a. Do you beat your wife enthusiastically?   (F-20)
    b. I don't beat my wife enthusiastically.

In Sentence a, we are not asking whether you beat your wife. We are assuming that you do, and we are asking whether you are enthusiastic in doing so. Note that a is synonymous with:

    Are you enthusiastic in beating your wife?   (F-21)

If we derive Sentence a of (F-20) from the structure underlying (F-21), we can account for the synonymy of the sentences. Otherwise, it is difficult to see how we could do so. In questions, it is usually the highest VP that we are questioning. If a of (F-20) had the underlying structure of (F-22),

                                     (F-22)

```
                         S
         _____|_____
        /           |                     |
        Q          NP                     VP
                    |            _____|_____
                    |           |       |          |
                    |           V      NP        Manner
                    |           |     /  \         |
                  You         beat your wife  enthusiastically
```

we would expect the a of (F-20) would be questioning whether the beating took place. Instead, it questions only the enthusiasm with which the beating occurs.

    Similarly, b of (F-20) does not deny that I beat my wife. It assumes that I do, and only denies that I do so with enthusiasm. Since negatives usually negate the uppermost VP, one would guess that if b of (F-20) had the deep structure of (F-23), then the beating would be denied.

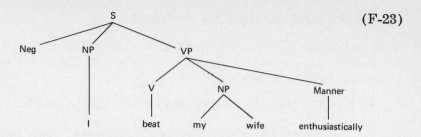

(F-23)

Note that b of (F-20) is synonymous with (F-24).

I'm not enthusiastic in beating my wife.   (F-24)

(F-24) has the deep structure:

(F-25)

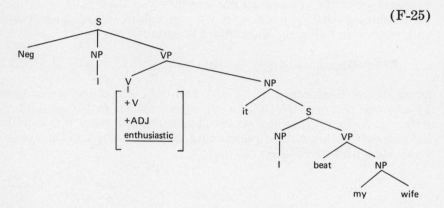

We can account for the meaning of b of (F-20) if we assume that it also has the deep structure of (F-25).

The same argument can be made in the case of imperatives. Consider the sentence:

Drive carefully.   (F-26)

(F-26) is *not* a command to drive. It is a command to be careful. Observe that (F-26) is synonymous with (F-27).

Be careful at driving.   (F-27)

We can account for these facts if we derive (F-26) from the structure underlying (F-27).

If we derive manner adverbials from adjectival complements, we can also account for the nonoccurrence of such commands as:

*Drive well. (F-28)

We would predict the nonoccurrence of (F-28) from the nonoccurrence of (F-29).

*Be good at driving. (F-29)

(F-29) does not occur because *good at* is a stative adjective, and statives do not take imperatives. Note that *careful* in (F-27) is nonstative.

One of the most interesting things about these examples is that embedded verbs, which are *not* associated with the question, negative, and imperative markers in the deep structure, come to be associated with them by transformation and then undergo the question, negative, and imperative transformations. Thus, underlying embedded verbs may come to be surface main verbs. As we shall see in the succeeding sections, this is an extremely common phenomenon.

F.5 LOCATIVE ADVERBIALS

Just as we brought forth arguments to show that manner adverbials are derived from a "higher" simplex sentence than the one that appears as the main clause in the surface structure, so we can bring forth the same arguments for deriving locative adverbials in this manner. Consider the sentence:

Do you beat your wife in the yard? (F-30)

(F-30) is not questioning whether the beating takes place. It assumes that it does, and it is questioning the location of the beating. (F-30) is synonymous with (F-31).

Is it in the yard that you beat your wife? (F-31)

In (F-31) it is clear in the surface structure that it is the location that is being questioned.

The same arguments hold for negatives. Consider

I don't beat my wife in the yard. (F-32)

In (F-32) it is again assumed that the beating does take place. What is denied is that the location of the beating is in the yard. Note that (F-32) is synonymous with (F-33).

It is not in the yard that I beat my wife. (F-33)

In (F-33) it is clear in the surface structure that the location of the event is being negated, not the assertion that the event occurs. [See Remark F-1.]

We can acount for all these facts if we derive (F-30) and (F-32) from the abstract structures underlying (F-31) and (F-33), respectively. The deep structure underlying (F-32) and (F-33) would, for example, be:

(F-34)

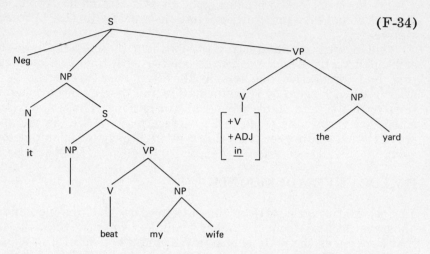

[As to the question of whether *in* is an adjective, see Section 10.2.] Observe that if extraposition operates and the embedded S is shifted to the end, we get (F-33). Since extraposition is an optional rule, it may not operate, in which case it-deletion obligatorily applies and yields (F-32). If this analysis is correct, the derived structure of (F-32) would be:

(F-35)

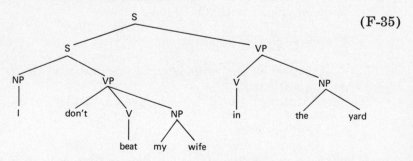

This differs substantially from the traditional surface analysis of the sentence, but it is by no means implausible, and seems quite defensible.

Note that we are claiming—also contrary to both traditional and recent transformational analysis—that the cleft sentence structure is basic and not derived in these cases. If the cleft sentence were derived, then we would expect the cleft sentence corresponding to *I don't beat my wife in the yard* to be

*It is in the yard that I don't beat my wife. (F-36)

Instead it is (F-33). Note that we can account for the nonoccurrence of (F-36) by the deep structure restriction (however it is to be formally stated) that one cannot assert the location of an event that did not occur.

F.6 REASON ADVERBIALS

Reason adverbials seem to be derived from "higher" simplex sentences in the same way as manner and locative adverbials are. Consider the question:

Do you beat your wife because you don't like her? (F-37)

(F-37) assumes that you beat your wife and is questioning your reason for doing so. (F-37) is synonymous with (F-38).

Is it because you don't like her that you beat your (F-38)
wife?

We can account for this if we derive (F-37) from the abstract structure underlying (F-38).

Only by deriving the *because*-clause from the VP. of a higher S can we account for the ambiguity of:

I don't beat my wife because I like her. (F-39)

The two senses of (F-39) are synonymous with those of (F-40) and (F-41):

It is because I like her that I don't beat my wife. (F-40)

It is not because I like her that I beat my wife. (F-41)

The only way that we could reasonably account for the ambiguity of (F-39) would be to derive it from the abstract structures underlying (F-40) and (F-41) [See Remark F-2]. These structures are:

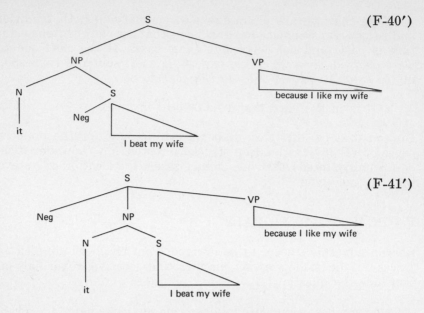

(F-40′)

(F-41′)

[See Remark F-3 for some discussion of the internal structure of the *because*-clause.]

Note that if extraposition does not take place, it-deletion occurs and, as a result, the structures will look almost identical.

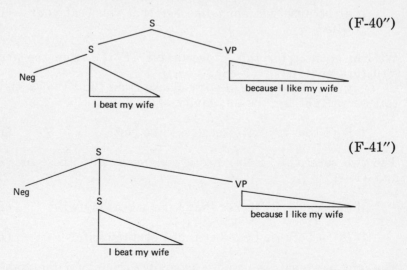

(F-40″)

(F-41″)

Beat will now be interpreted as the main verb of the sentence, and NEG will attach itself to *beat* in both cases. Observe that in order for *beat* to be characterized as the main verb in these sentences, we will have to revise our notion of main verb. Rather than defining the main verb as the highest V in the P-marker, we will define it as the highest V that has a noun phrase subject.

F.7 INSTRUMENTAL ADVERBIALS

The same arguments that we have given in the preceeding sections apply to instrumental adverbials. Consider the question:

Do you beat your wife with a whip? (F-42)

(F-42) assumes that you beat your wife and is questioning whether you use a whip in doing so. (F-42) is synonymous with (F-43).

Is it with a whip that you beat your wife? (F-43)

We can account for the way in which we understand (F-42) if we derive it from the abstract structure underlying (F-43).
Now consider the sentence:

I don't beat my wife with a whip. (F-44)

(F-44) assumes that I beat my wife and only denies that I use a whip to do so. (F-44) is synonymous with (F-45).

It is not with a whip that I beat my wife. (F-45)

We can account for the way in which we understand (F-44) by deriving it from the structure underlying (F-45). Note that (F-45) not (F-46) is the cleft sentence corresponding to (F-44).

*It is with a whip that I don't beat my wife. (F-46)

The nonoccurrence of (F-46) follows from a deep structure restriction (however it is to be stated) that one cannot assert that one uses an instrument in an activity which one does not perform.

F.8 FREQUENCY ADVERBIALS

Consider the question:

Do you beat your wife often? (F-47)

(F-47) assumes that you beat your wife and questions whether the occurrence is frequent. (F-47) is synonymous with (F-48).

Is it often that you beat your wife?   (F-48)

We can account for the way in which we understand (F-47) by deriving it from the abstract structure underlying (F-48).
    Now consider:

I don't beat my wife often.   (F-49)

(F-49) assumes that I do beat my wife, but denies that I do so frequently. (F-49) is synonymous with (F-50).

It is not often that I beat my wife.   (F-50)

Again, we can account for our understanding of (F-49) by deriving it from the structure underlying (F-50). And again observe that (F-50) and not (F-51) is the cleft sentence corresponding to (F-49).

*It is often that I don't beat my wife.   (F-51)

(F-51) does not occur because one cannot assert the frequency of an event that does not occur. (F-52) is ruled out for the same reason.

*I don't beat my wife seldom.   (F-52)

    We would set up the following deep structure for (F-47) and (F-48):

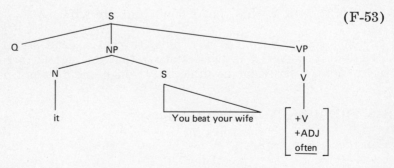

(F-53)

If extraposition occurs, we get (F-48). Otherwise, it-deletion occurs and we get (F-47). Note that it-deletion yields the following structure:

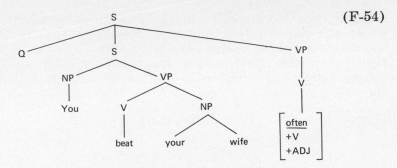

(F-54)

Note that the deletion of the node NP dominating *it* now makes *beat* the main verb according to our definition in Section F.6. Thus, *beat,* the embedded verb in the deep structure, will undergo the question transformation.

F.9 QUANTIFIERS

So far, we have shown that what have been called main clauses in traditional grammar very often arise as embedded clauses and assume their stature as main clauses only through transformational derivation. The examples that we have dealt with thus far have all contained what have traditionally been called adverbials. We have presented evidence to show that these "adverbials" are derived from verb phrases of simplex sentences which are higher in the base phrase marker than the supposed main clauses. We will now consider another case of the same sort.

In traditional studies, as well as in recent transformational ones, quantifiers have been analyzed as being constituents of the noun phrases that they quantify. A typical recent analysis is that given in the Mitre Grammar. The Mitre grammarians analyze quantifiers as being introduced in a prearticle constituent, which is itself a constituent of the determiner. That is, they propose that quantified noun phrases have the following underlying constituent structure:

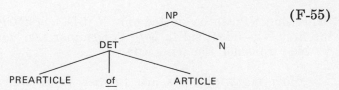

(F-55)

This structure would underlie *two of the boys* and *how many of the boys* when the article is definite. When the article is indefinite, the Mitre grammarians assume, *it* and *of* are transformationally deleted. Thus, the structure in (F-55) with an indefinite article would underlie *two boys* and *how many boys*. The Mitre grammarians also assume that *many* always appears in the underlying structure whenever an integer appears. Thus, they would have the prearticle consisting of a degree constituent followed by *many*.

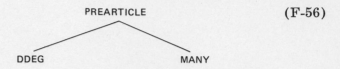

PREARTICLE   (F-56)

DDEG   MANY

Thus, *two of the boys* would be derived from *two many of the boys* by the deletion of *many* and so it would be completely parallel to *how many of the boys*, where the *many* is not deleted.

The inadequacy of the view that quantifiers appear in the deep structure as constituents of the noun phrases that they quantify can be seen clearly in the comparative construction. As Robert Lees [1961] pointed out, a sentence such as

This airport is further from New York than from   (F-57)
Chicago.

must, at some point in its derivation, have as its terminal string:

This airport is more far from New York than this   (F-58)
airport is far from Chicago.

By a transformational rule, the second occurrence of *this airport* will be deleted if it is identical with the first occurrence of *this airport*. This is in general the case in the derivation of comparatives. Whenever we have

NP is more far from New York than NP is far from   (F-59)
Chicago.

the second NP can be deleted only if it is *completely identical* with the first NP—identical in *both* determiner and noun.

Now consider the sentence:

How many airports are further from New York   (F-60)
than from Chicago?

If *how many* is introduced as a constituent of the noun phrase containing *airports*, then (F-60) must, at some point in its derivation, have the terminal string:

Q *how many airports* are more far from New York   (F-61)
than *how many airports* are far from Chicago.

The noun phrase containing *airports* must appear *twice* in the deep structure underlying the comparative sentence (F-60). Thus, it follows from the assumption that quantifiers are introduced as deep structure constituents of the noun phrases they quantify that the quantifier *how many* must occur *twice* in the deep structure of (F-60). This is clearly absurd.

There should be only one occurrence of *how many* in the deep structure of sentences like (F-60). We can provide an analysis of (F-60) that meets this condition if we treat *many* as an adjective of the same sort as *long, numerous,* and so on. Consider the following sentences:

How long are the airports that are further from   (F-62)
New York than from Chicago?

How numerous are the airports that are further   (F-63)
from New York than from Chicago?

Observe that (F-63) is synonymous with (F-60). Also observe that the parallel sentence with *many* sounds more archaic than ungrammatical.

How many are the airports that are further from   (F-64)
New York than from Chicago?

(F-64) is similar to such archaisms as (F-65) and (F-66).

How many are the stars in the sky?   (F-65)
Many were the times that I held her in my arms.   (F-66)

If we assume that the rule which accounts for the generation of (F-60) rather than (F-64) was once optional and is now obligatory, we can account for these familiar archaisms. Such a rule would assume a deep structure like (F-67).

(F-67)

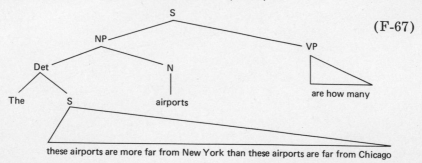

these airports are more far from New York than these airports are far from Chicago

Exactly what such a rule would look like would depend upon the analysis of predicates containing measure adjectives and their quantifiers that we choose to adopt. We do not take any position on that matter here. But given any adequate analysis of predicates containing measure adjectives and their quantifiers, we can treat *many* as a measure adjective and set up a rule that shifts the constituent containing QUANTIFIER + *many* into the determiner of the subject noun phrase. (The same analysis would hold for *much*.) Observe that since measure adjective quantification must be accounted for anyway, we can reduce noun phrase quantification to a case of measure adjective quantification. And rather than having two sources of quantifier (in noun phrases and with measure adjectives), we would now have only one.

This analysis of noun phrase quantifier is corroborated by the way that we understand sentences like (F-68).

Not much shrapnel hit the soldier.   (F-68)

(F-68) has the passive (F-69).

The soldier was not hit by much shrapnel.   (F-69)

These sentences do not deny that the soldier was hit. Rather, they assert that the soldier was hit by some shrapnel. They only deny that the amount of shrapnel that hit the soldier was much.

Similarly, consider the questions, (F-70) and (F-71).

Did much shrapnel hit the soldier?   (F-70)
Was the soldier hit by much shrapnel?   (F-71)

These sentences do not question whether or not the soldier was hit. They again assume that the soldier was hit by some shrapnel, and they question the amount.

We can account for the way in which we understand these sentences, if we derive (F-68) and (F-69) from (F-72) and if we derive (F-70) and (F-71) from (F-73).

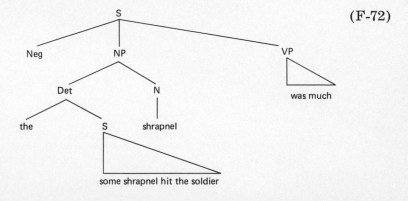

(F-72)

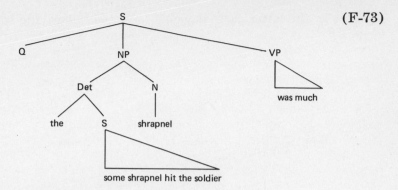

(F-73)

Since all quantifiers will now occur in predicates we should not be surprised to find quantifiers occurring in embedded clauses as well as in matrix clauses. For example, consider:

The firing squad executed two students.　　　　(F-74)

(F-74) would have the deep structure:

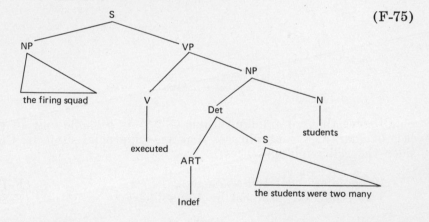

(F-75)

Since noun phrase quantifiers may be derived either from "higher" sentences containing quantifier predicates or from embedded relative clauses of the same sort, one would expect to find cases of ambiguity—where a single noun phrase quantifier can be derived from two such underlying sources. Consider the sentence:

Did many inmates escape?　　　　(F-76)

(F-76) may either be questioning whether an escape by many inmates took place or it may be assuming that some inmates escaped and questioning whether the number that escaped was great. In the former case, (F-76) would have the deep structure of

(F-77). In the latter case, it would have the underlying structure
of (F-78).

(F-77)

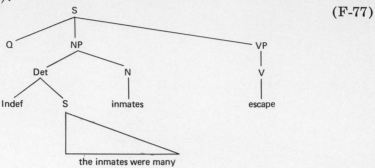

(F-78)

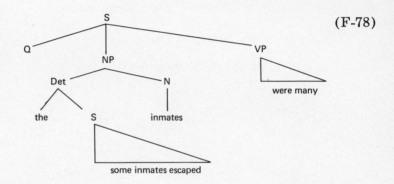

Observe that an ambiguity like (F-76) is possible only in the
case of quantified noun phrases that are superficial subjects. Consider the following sentences:

100 soldiers shot two students. (F-79)
Two students were shot by 100 soldiers. (F-80)

(F-79) has the following interpretations:

a. A group of soldiers, who were 100 in number, shot a total
   of two students.
b. 100 soldiers (perhaps out of a larger group) shot two
   students apiece, though not the same two students.

(F-80) has interpretation a, which we might paraphrase as:

a′. A total of two students were shot by a group of soldiers,
    which numbered 100.

But (F-80) is not open to interpretation b. Instead it has interpretation c.

  c. Two particular students (out of all those that were shot) were each shot by 100 soldiers (though not necessarily by the same 100).

These correspond to the following underlying structures:

a.

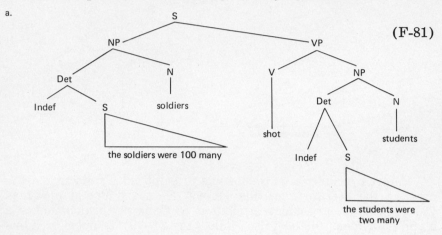

(F-81)

b.

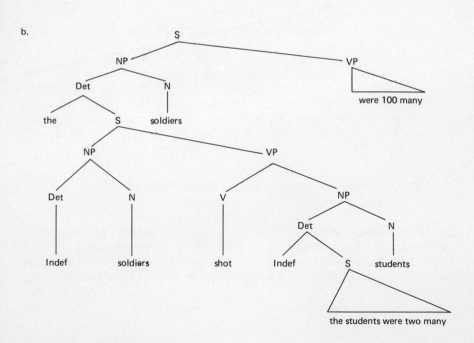

c.

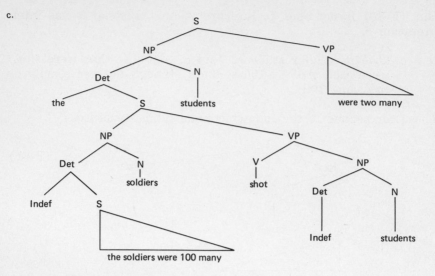

Before concluding, we would like to point out a fallacious argument in the literature on this subject. Katz and Postal [1964, p. 73] present an argument attributed to Chomsky which makes a claim equivalent to the false claim that (F-79) is open to interpretation c. The sentence in question is:

Everyone in the room knows two languages.   (F-82)

The claim is that (F-82) is open to the interpretation that everyone in the room knows two particular languages, say, Mohawk and Hebrew. The argument proceeds as follows: The assumption is made, though not explicitly written down, that quantifiers are introduced in the deep structure as constituents of the noun phrases that they quantify. The following sentence is then considered:

There are two languages which everyone in the room   (F-83)
      knows.

In (F-83) there is no question that two *particular* languages are referred to. The assumption is then made that *which* in (F-83) must have been derived from an underlying *two languages*, that is, a noun phrase with a quantifier inside of it. The structure they assume is:

(F-84)

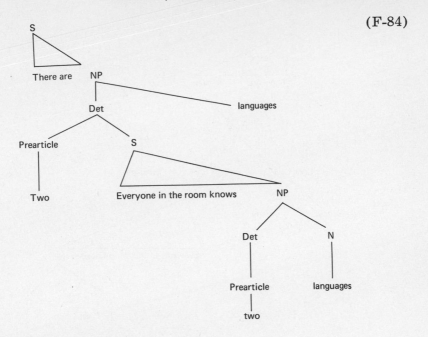

They then reason that since the uppermost occurrence of *two languages* refers to particular languages, so the embedded occurrence of *two languages* must do the same.

The flaw in the reasoning is the *assumption* that quantifiers are deep structure constituents of the noun phrases they quantify. Note the consequences of this line of reasoning for sentences like (F-83). Consider (F-85), the question corresponding to (F-83):

How many languages are there which everyone in   (F-85)
this room knows?

Since *how many* must be introduced in the same constituent as *two, how many* must be a deep structure constituent (say, prearticle) of the noun phrase *how many languages*. Since *which* in (F-83) is a reduced form of the noun phrase *two languages,* it follows that *which* in (F-85) is a reduced form of the noun phrase *how many languages.* That is, the deep structure of (F-85) must contain *two* occurrences of *how many:*

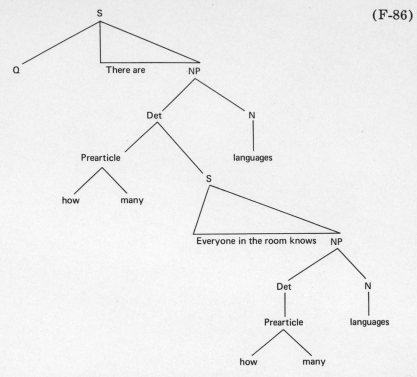

(F-86)

This is just as absurd as the claim that there are two occurrences of *how many* in the deep structure underlying (F-60). Actually the deep structures underlying (F-83) and (F-85) are (F-87) and (F-88), respectively.

(F-87)

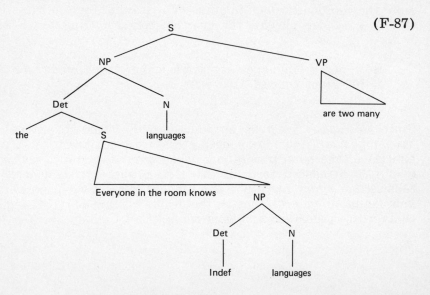

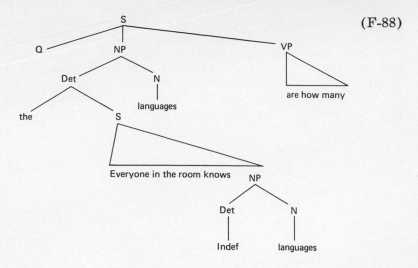

(F-88)

F.10 MULTIPLE ADVERBIALS

It has often been noted that in sentences with more than one adverbial a change in the order of the adverbials may produce a considerable change in the meaning of the sentence. Consider the following sentences:

> I beat my wife often because she serves red wine (F-89)
> with fish.
> I often beat my wife because she serves red wine (F-90)
> with fish.

In (F-89) I am telling the reason why I beat my wife often. In (F-90) I am telling the frequency with which I beat my wife because she serves red wine with fish. This distinction shows up quite clearly in the corresponding questions:

> Do you beat your wife often because she serves red (F-91)
> wine with fish?
> Do you often beat your wife because she serves red (F-92)
> wine with fish?

(F-91) assumes that you beat your wife often and is questioning your reason for doing so. (F-92) assumes that you beat your wife because she serves red wine with fish and is questioning how often you do so.

As we pointed out in the preceding sections, reason and frequency adverbials must be introduced as the verb phrases of "higher" simplex sentences than the superficial main clause. Recall that the main clause of the surface structure was embedded in the deep structure subject of the verb phrase which became a derived adverbial. We can account for the occurrence of multiple adverbials and for the way that we understand them if we assume that sentences containing adverbials may be embedded into the subjects of other "adverbial" verb phrases. Thus, we can account for the different questions of (F-91) and (F-92) by assuming that they are derived from the following deep structures:

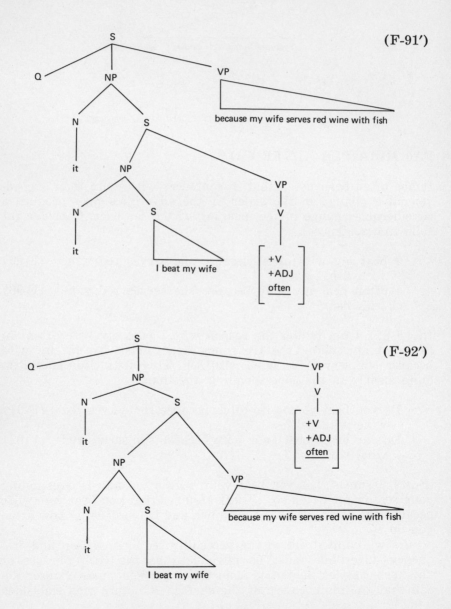

(F-91')

(F-92')

Observe that it is only when *often* is the highest VP in the tree that it can be moved to the position following the superficial subject. For example, a and b of (F-93) are synonymous with each other, but not with (F-94).

a. I beat my wife in public often.   (F-93)
b. I often beat my wife in public.

I beat my wife often in public.   (F-94)

(F-94) asserts the place where I beat my wife often. (F-93) asserts the frequency with which I beat my wife in public. They would have the following deep structures:

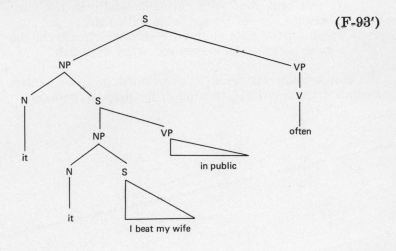

(F-93′)

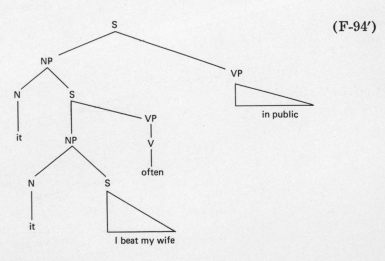

(F-94′)

Note that in a of (F-93) and in (F-94) the linear order of the adverbs reflects their relative heights in the underlying P-markers. In b of (F-93) *often* appears after the superficial subject. Since b of (F-93) is synonymous with a of (F-93) but not with (F-94), we can only conclude that *often* can be moved to this position when it is the highest VP in the P-marker and that the transformation which shifts *often* to this position is postcyclical.

The occurrence of many adverbials within a sentence often reflects a rather deep level of embedding. Consider the following sentences:

Do you beat your wife enthusiastically?	(F-95)
Do you beat your wife enthusiastically in the yard?	(F-96)
Do you beat your wife enthusiastically in the yard because she serves red wine with fish?	(F-97)
Do you often beat your wife enthusiastically in the yard because she serves red wine with fish?	(F-98)

We can account for what is questioned in these sentences if we assume that they have the following deep structures:

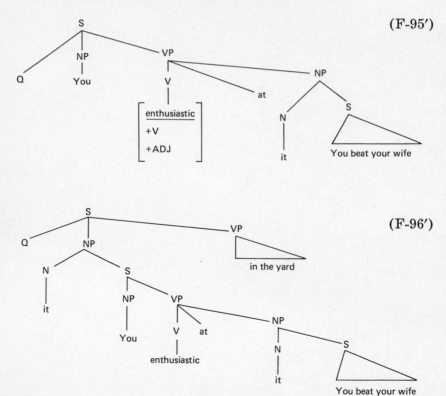

(F-95′)

(F-96′)

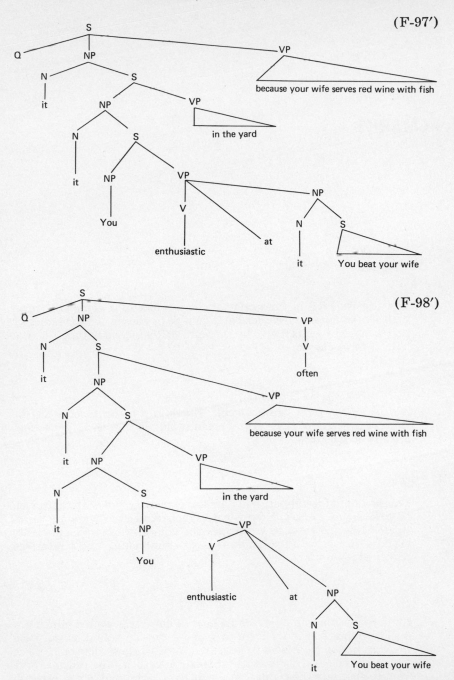

(F-97′)

(F-98′)

Observe that in (F-95), (F-96), and (F-97) the linear order of the adverbials exactly mirrors their relative depths of embedding.

REMARKS

R 1-1

The feature PRO in the grammatical member of a complex symbol indicates whether or not a lexical item is to be chosen. +PRO indicates that a lexical item is *not* to be chosen. −PRO indicates that a lexical item *is* to be chosen.

R 4-1

My use of the term "government" should not be confused with the traditional usage of that term. I mean it only in the special sense that I define on page 28.

R 5-1

This account of it-substitution does not exactly accord with that given by Rosenbaum [1967]. However, the facts which motivate my treatment of this phenomenon are largely the same as those which motivate his. His discussion of the topic is most enlightening and I refer the reader to his work.

R 5-2

By hypothesizing an abstract inchoative pro-verb, we are making a weaker claim than if we were to suppose that an actual lexical item (such as *get* or *come about*) appeared in the deep structure of these sentences. The abstract nature of this pro-verb will be crucial if we want to maintain the claim that a transformation may not substitute one lexical item for another, except under identity.

R   5-3

For the sake of exposition, we have included in our "underlying" structures items that really are transformationally introduced, for instance, the "for-to" complementizer. If we were to be precise in using our notion of underlying structure, we would represent (5-19) as follows:

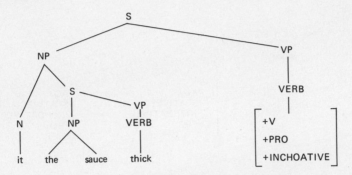

R   5-4

Let us consider the operation of the inchoative transformation in some greater detail. (5-23), with relevant details included, would appear as follows:

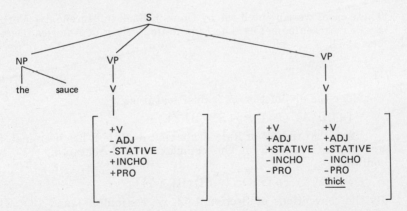

Note that, by this time, all of the *m*'s and *u*'s that appeared in the lexical entry for *thick* have been converted into pluses and minuses. We assume that this process took place *before* any transformations applied, that is, that the above features determine *deep structure distribution* and that possible violations with respect to these features are determined on the deep structure level. Note also that no lexical item has been chosen for the lexical member of the inchoative proverb. The inchoative transformation will substitute the lexical mem-

ber of the adjective into the slot for the lexical member of the inchoative pro-verb. The adjective will then be deleted, yielding:

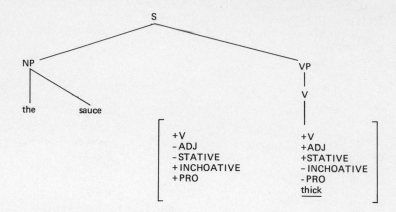

Note that, although most of the features of the grammatical member
no longer match those of the lexical member, there will be no violation,
since possible violations for those features are defined only on the
level of deep structure.

R 6-1

These cases were pointed out by Emmon Bach in "Irreflexive Verbs,"
a paper presented before The Linguistic Society of America, December, 1964.

R 7-1

Consider the disjunction of lexical features:

$$[+SD(A)\ (L)] \lor [+SD(B)\ (L)] \tag{1}$$

If neither the SD of Rule A nor that of Rule B has been met, the
grammatical member of the complex symbol containing (1) will
contain:

$$[-SD(A)\ (G)]\ \text{and}\ [-SD(B)\ (G)] \tag{2}$$

By the conventions of Section 1.52, we conjoin (1) and (2). This
yields:

$$[-SD(A)\ (G)]\ \text{and}\ [-SD(B)\ (G)]\ \text{and} \tag{3}$$

$$\overline{[+SD(A)\ (L)] \lor [+SD(B)\ (L)]}$$

By the distributive law of elementary logic, we get:

$$\overline{[-SD(A)\ (G)]\ \text{and}\ [-SD(B)\ (G)]\ \text{and}\ [+SD(A)\ (L)]} \lor \tag{4}$$

$$\overline{[-SD(A)\ (G)]\ \text{and}\ [-SD(B)\ (G)]\ \text{and}\ [+SD(B)\ (L)]}$$

If we map the G features into the L features, we will obliterate the distinction at this point and get:

$$\overline{[-SD(A)] \text{ and } [-SD(B)] \text{ and } [+SD(A)]} \lor \qquad (5)$$
$$\overline{[-SD(A)] \text{ and } [-SD(B)] \text{ and } [+SD(B)]}$$

Recall that $[-F] \equiv \sim [+F]$ for all features, F. Thus (5) is equivalent to:

$$\overline{\sim[+SD(B)] \text{ and } \sim[+SD(A)] \text{ and } [+SD(A)]} \lor \qquad (6)$$
$$\overline{\sim[+SD(A)] \text{ and } \sim[+SD(B)] \text{ and } [+SD(B)]}$$

Each member of the disjunction contains a contradiction of the form: $\sim[F]$ and $[F]$. Hence we get a contradiction for the entire disjunction, and by Section 1.52, a violation. Note that if (2) had contained a plus-valued SD feature, no violation would have resulted.

R 8-1

The fact that we can get *the boy who is content* but not either **the boy content* or **the content boy* seems to indicate that *content* is a simple exception to the optional rule WH-DEL—that is, it may not undergo that rule. However, this analysis cannot be maintained in the face of examples such as *the boy content with his lot* which must be derived from *the boy who is content with his lot*. This shows that *content* may undergo WH-DEL. *Content* is surely an exceptional lexical item. Let us raise the question of just what kind of exception *content* is.

Consider the following sentences:

    I. A. Exceptional Adjectives
          1. a. I know a boy who is *content* with his lot.
            b. I know a boy *content* with his lot.
            c. I know a boy who is *content*.
            d. *I know a boy *content*.
            e. *I know a *content* boy.
          2. a. I knew a murderer who was *sorry* about what he had done.
            b. I knew a murderer *sorry* about what he had done.
            c. I knew a murderer who was *sorry*.
            d. *I knew a murderer *sorry*.
            e. *I knew a *sorry* murderer.
          3. a. I know a girl who is *ready* to enter college.
            b. I know a girl *ready* to enter college.
            c. I know a girl who is *ready*.
            d. *I know a girl *ready*.
            e. *I know a *ready* girl.

    I. B. Ordinary Adjectives
          1. a. I know a boy who is *satisfied* with his lot.
            b. I know a boy *satisfied* with his lot.

    c. I know a boy who is *satisfied*.
    d. *I know a boy *satisfied*.
    e. I know a *satisfied* boy.
   2. a. I knew a murderer who was *repentant* about what
     he had done.
    b. I knew a murderer *repentant* about what he had
     done.
    c. I knew a murderer who was *repentant*.
    d. *I knew a murderer *repentant*.
    e. I knew a *repentant* murderer.
   3. a. I know a girl who is *anxious* about entering college.
    b. I know a girl *anxious* about entering college.
    c. I know a girl who is *anxious*.
    d. *I know a girl *anxious*.
    e. I know an *anxious* girl.

As we pointed out in Section 5.3, ordinary adjectives do undergo ADJ-SHIFT, while exceptional ones do not. On the other hand, ordinary verbs do *not* undergo ADJ-SHIFT, while exceptional ones do.

  II. A. Ordinary Verbs
   1. a. I knew the man who was *shot* in the subway.
    b. I knew the man *shot* in the subway.
    c. I knew the man who was *shot*.
    d. *I knew the man *shot*.
    e. *I knew the *shot* man.
   2. a. The bracelet that was *bought* by Harry was
     returned.
    b. The bracelet *bought* by Harry was returned.
    c. The bracelet that was *bought* was returned.
    d. *The bracelet *bought* was returned.
    e. *The *bought* bracelet was returned.
   3. a. Looney was an official who was *chosen* by a large
     majority.
    b. Looney was an official *chosen* by a large majority.
    c. Looney was an official who was *chosen*.
    d. *Looney was an official *chosen*.
    e. *Looney was a *chosen* official.

  II. B. Exceptional Verbs
   1. a. I knew the man who was *murdered* in the subway.
    b. I knew the man *murdered* in the subway.
    c. I knew the man who was *murdered*.
    d. *I knew the man *murdered*.
    e. I knew the *murdered* man.
   2. a. The bracelet that was *stolen* by Harry was
     returned.
    b. The bracelet *stolen* by Harry was returned.
    c. The bracelet that was *stolen* was returned.
    d. *The bracelet *stolen* was returned.
    e. The *stolen* bracelet was returned.

3. a. Looney was an official who was *elected* by a large majority.
   b. Looney was an official *elected* by a large majority.
   c. Looney was an official who was *elected*.
   d. *Looney was an official *elected*.
   e. Looney was an *elected* official.

Recall from Section A.4 that ADJ-SHIFT applies to structures of the form:

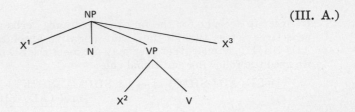

(III. A.)

and maps them into structures of the form:

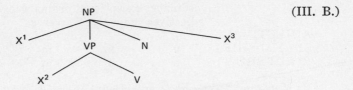

(III. B.)

where X^1, X^2, and X^3 are (possibly null) variables

Note that in the b sentences above the SD will not be met since the verbs and adjectives in question are not the final constituents of VP. What happens in the case of exceptional adjectives and ordinary verbs is that if the structural description of ADJ-SHIFT is met at all, a violation results whether or not ADJ-SHIFT actually applies. Hence, the d and e sentences of I.A and II.A are all ungrammatical.

We can account for these facts in the following way. Assume that ordinary and exceptional verbs and adjectives are represented in the following fashion:

	1 ordinary adjectives	2 exceptional adjectives	3 ordinary verbs	4 exceptional verbs	(IV)
ADJECTIVAL	+	+	−	−	
SD(ADJ-SHIFT)	u	u	u	u	
R(ADJ-SHIFT)	u	m	u	m	

Note from I and II above that exceptional verbs act just like ordinary adjectives, and that ordinary verbs act just like exceptional adjectives. We can express this fact by considering ADJ-SHIFT as a rule which is minor for verbs. The following rule will state this:

$$[\gamma\ R(\text{ADJ-SHIFT})] \rightarrow [\sim\gamma\ R(\text{ADJ-SHIFT})]\ / \qquad\qquad (V)$$
$$[-\text{ADJECTIVAL}]$$

(V) will map the values given in (IV) into those given in (VI).

	1 ordinary adjectives	2 exceptional adjectives	3 ordinary verbs	4 exceptional verbs	(VI)
ADJECTIVAL	+	+	−	−	
SD(ADJ-SHIFT)	u	u	u	u	
R(ADJ-SHIFT)	u	m	m	u	

In order to account for the fact that ordinary verbs and exceptional adjectives act as though they were negative absolute exceptions to ADJ-SHIFT, namely, that they may not meet the SD of ADJ-SHIFT, we need the following additional rule:

$$[\text{u SD}(\text{ADJ-SHIFT})] \rightarrow [\text{m SD}(\text{ADJ-SHIFT})]\ / \qquad (VII)$$
$$[\text{m R}\ (\text{ADJ-SHIFT})]$$

(VII) will map the values given in (VI) into those given in (VIII).

	1 ordinary adjectives	2 exceptional adjectives	3 ordinary verbs	4 exceptional verbs	(VIII)
ADJECTIVAL	+	+	−	−	
SD(ADJ-SHIFT)	u	m	m	u	
R(ADJ-SHIFT)	u	m	m	u	

By Metarules 1 through 5, exceptional adjectives and ordinary verbs will be treated as negative absolute exceptions to ADJ-SHIFT, while ordinary adjectives and exceptional verbs will be treated as normal cases with respect to that rule.

R   10-1

As we noted above, *convince* and *persuade* are parallel cases. In both traditional and transformational treatments of English, these verbs have regularly been grouped together, and it is assumed that they are to be treated in the same way. We agree with these observations and our analysis is in accord with them. Note, however, that *convince* appears in a form that *persuade* does not appear in:

1. John is convinced that there is no God.
2. *John is persuaded that there is no God.

Sentence 1 does not entail that someone has convinced John; that is, there is no causative agent present. Thus 1 cannot have been derived from a sentence like 3, which contains the causative sense of *convince*, by means of the passive transformation.

3. Someone convinced John that there is no God.

Moreover, the fact that 1 appears in the present tense provides an independent argument against its derivation by means of the passive transformation from the causative sense of *convince*, since neither nonstative verb nor its passive may occur in the simple present. Thus, we get neither 4 nor 5 (except in the historical present).

4. *Someone convinces John that there is no God.
5. *John is convinced by someone that there is no God.

Thus, *convince* in 1 seems to be an underlying form. Its meaning is "to believe strongly"—exactly the same underlying meaning that we had to postulate for the causatives *convince* and *persuade*. If we permit the existence of hypothetical verbs, then we can maintain our analysis of *convince* and *persuade* as being synonyms that enter into parallel derivations. We can account for the occurrence of 1 by representing *convince* with a slightly different lexical extension than *persuade*. Since *convince* may undergo the causative transformation, but need not do so, it will not be represented as an absolute exception to causative. *Convince* will differ from *persuade* in that *convince* will contain the feature [u SD (CAUSATIVE)] where *persuade* contains the feature [m SD (CAUSATIVE)].

In any theory of grammar that *excludes* hypothetical lexical items, *convince* and *persuade* will have to be given strikingly different lexical representations, and sentences like

6. Bill convinced John that there is no God.
7. Bill persuaded John that there is no God.

will have to be derived in entirely different ways. In order to show the obvious relationship between 6 and 1, we will have to derive 6 by the causative transformation from a deep structure with causative pro-verb as main verb and with the underlying structure of 1 embedded within it. If no hypothetical lexical items are permitted, then *persuade* will have to be represented in the lexicon as some sort of lexical causative. Sentence 7 will have an entirely different deep structure than 6 and will be derived in an entirely different manner.

R   10-2

Suppose that someone were to devise a theory of language that would somehow exclude hypothetical lexical items. Then, as we pointed out in Remark 10-1, presumably parallel sentences containing *convince* and *persuade* [for example, 6 and 7 of Remark 10-1] would have to be derived from entirely different deep structures in any grammar of English. This means that the semantic component of English would need to contain, in general, two different rules of semantic interpretation for causatives—one for lexical causatives (*persuade* would have to be analyzed as such) and one for derived causatives (such as *convince*). Moreover, the semantic component in a grammar defined by such a theory would have to contain special "entailment rules" to account for such typical facts as: *Bill persuaded John to go* entails that at some point in time John intended to go. Such facts are accounted for automatically in our treatment of causatives, since an S with the meaning of "John intended to go" occurs embedded in the underlying structure of *Bill persuaded John to go.*

We have been assuming that it is possible to constrain a theory of language in a well-motivated way so as to rule out the occurrence of hypothetical verbs while still maintaining descriptive adequacy. In Chapters 6 and 10, we argued that this is not possible. But even if our arguments there were wrong, it is not apparent that one could find a well-motivated formal mechanism for ruling out hypothetical lexical items. Since any descriptively adequate theory must contain devices like SD features for handling absolute exceptions [see Sections 6.1 and 6.2], any such theory will automatically define a host of hypothetical lexical items other than the particular cases that the SD feature theory was set up to handle. Of course, it is always possible that one could rule out hypothetical lexical items by defining an evaluation measure of some kind that would make SD features very costly. Yet the matter of ruling out *all* hypothetical lexical items on principle (if one could ever find a justification for doing such a thing) seems to be a matter of restricting the form of a linguistic theory, rather than a matter of choosing the best grammar defined within a theory of a certain form. It is not at all clear how restrictions of *form* might be placed on a theory of language to exclude hypothetical lexical items, while permitting other sorts of absolute exceptions.

R 11-1

The lexical base hypothesis is a reformulation of my earlier position that certain (not all) features introduced in the base component are predictable on a one-one basis from semantic markers. Among these, I included ANIMATE, ABSTRACT, __NP, ANIMATE__, __ABSTRACT, STATIVE, and so on. This position, like my present one, was designed to account for the fact that the meaning of a word provided some (but by no means all) syntactic information about the word. However, since the nature of semantic markers is not well known, and since our intuitions about what constitutes a semantic marker are not clear, it seems desirable to state this position without tying it to any specific concept of semantic marker. In the formulation of the lexical base hypothesis, we have eliminated reference to semantic markers and have retreated to the notion of lexical synonymy— something that we have much clearer intuitions about. At the same time, we have moved from the position of listing one by one the features that we think are predictable from semantic information to the stronger position that all lexical base features must be predictable from semantic information. This latter position is probably much too strong. The feature ADJECTIVAL is a good case in point. *"Know about"* and *"be cognizant of"* are probably synonymous, but one is a verb, while the other is an adjective. If it is reasonable to assume that ADJECTIVAL is a lexical base feature, this case would constitute a counterexample to the lexical base hypothesis. This indicates that the hypothesis will probably have to be weakened in the following way: There will be two kinds of lexical base features—those that are "semantically rooted" and those that are not. At present, there seems to be no general principle to determine which features are semantically rooted, and which are not. In this case, the semantically rooted ones will simply have to be listed in our linguistic theory. This is unfortunate from an esthetic point of view, but certainly not without parallel. In phonology, certain feature values (for example, +STRIDENT) may not occur in any language with certain combinations of other feature values (for example, +VOCALIC, −CONSONANTAL). There seem to be no general principles about the nature of phonological features or about the form of grammars from which we could predict this. It is simply a fact, and all such cases must be listed in our theory of language. The same would be the case with semantically-rooted lexical base features. Our position then would be that two synonyms would have to have the same semantically-rooted lexical base features. This position, like the lexical base hypothesis, avoids any dependence on a particular view of what semantic markers are like.

R 11-2

Let us consider an example of the type of lexical base evidence that might have some bearing on the choice of one particular set of base rules over another. Rosenbaum [1965] proposed that the base component of English should characterize the following predicate complement structures:

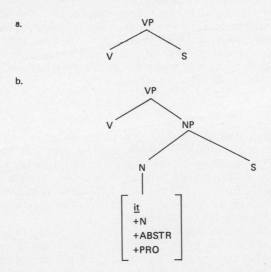

Verbs appearing in the configuration of a would contain the feature: [+__S]. Verbs appearing in the configuration of b would contain the features: [+__NP] and [+__[+N, +Abstr]].

As it turned out, Rosenbaum's arguments for the existence of the a complements were far from overwhelming. His major argument for the existence of a complements depended on the existence of a handful of verbs in English that can take predicate complements but not object nouns. Note that we can account for these verbs in another way. We can assume that they take complements of type b and that they are absolute exceptions to IT-DEL. Since they would have to meet the SD of IT-DEL, they could not take object nouns, and since the node NP in b would be deleted in the application of IT-DEL, the *derived* structure containing these verbs would be exactly a. Thus there are at least two ways of accounting for this handful of verbs, and there seems to be little to choose between them.

Now suppose that we assumed the lexical base hypothesis. Suppose, also, that for each verb that appeared to take an a complement, there existed a synonymous verb (either in English or in some other language) that could take *both* predicate complements and object nouns. That verb would have to appear in the configuration of b and would have to contain the lexical base features: [+__NP] and [+__[+N, +Abstr]]. By the lexical base hypothesis, the corresponding English verb would have to contain the same features and so would have to be analyzed as occurring in the b configurations and as being an absolute exception to IT-DEL. If one could make the same case for each such verb in each language that appeared to occur in the a configurations, then one could eliminate configurations like a from the universal base component. Thus, it is possible that the universal base hypothesis, coupled with interlingual evidence about lexical base features, *could* provide arguments in favor of one particular universal base over another.

All of this is, of course, sheer speculation. The lexical base hypothesis may be totally false, as may be the universal base hypothesis. But if these hypotheses were to turn out to be true, they would explain a great deal about natural language and would undoubtedly involve us in rethinking a great many of the grammatical analyses that have been carried out to date.

R   C-1

Preliminary studies within a generative phonological framework of languages with voiceless vowels have shown that voicelessness in vowels seems to be predictable by phonological rules, and that therefore these languages do not have voiceless vowels as systematic phonemes. If further study should show that no known language has voiceless vowels as systematic phonemes, then this would turn out to be a bad example for our purposes.

An adequate example for our purposes, though one which is less obvious and by no means certain, would concern compactness in vowels and consonants. So far as we can tell at present, vowels unmarked for compactness are compact, vowels marked for compactness are noncompact; the opposite is true for consonants. The evidence is as follows: The neutral position of the vocal tract in the production of vowels is compact. In the production of stop consonants, the neutral position is noncompact. Corresponding to this is the fact that children learn to produce compact vowels before noncompact ones, and they learn to produce noncompact stops before compact ones (hence, *ma-ma, pa-pa, da-da*, and so on). Moreover, in positions of neutralization, vowels tend to become compact (schwa). One can make a weaker case for the tendency of neutralized consonants to be noncompact. In languages where there is only one nasal systematic phoneme, it is common for that nasal to assimilate before stop consonants, but for it to appear as *n* in neutral position: intervocalically and at the end of words. One can also cite the example of Finnish, where final consonants become dental. However, all the facts are by no means in, and those that are are by no means conclusive.

R   C-2

Perhaps we ought to reiterate what we mean by "normal." We can speak of the normal value of a feature only with respect to other given values of other features. Thus, given that a segment is a vowel, we say that it is "normal" for it to have the value + with respect to the feature VOICED. Given that a segment is a consonant, we say that it is "normal" for it to have the value − with respect to the feature NASAL. Given that a segment is a consonant and −CONTINUANT, we say that it is normal for it to have the value − with respect to the feature STRIDENT. Thus, the notion of normality assumes the existence of a hierarchy of features such that for any given feature normality can be defined only with respect to some combination of features higher up in the hierarchy.

As the development of theory of generative phonology is now envisioned, distinctive features should be made to correlate more and more closely to the significant deformations of the human vocal tract for the production of speech sounds. In essence, features should be physiologically as well as acoustically based, with "significant deformation" to be defined with respect to the phonological phenomena found in empirical studies of natural languages. The notion of "normality" is envisioned as correlating with the physiological notion of "ease of production" with respect to the human vocal tract in general, rather than the ease of an adult speaking a particular language. Thus, when we say that it is "normal" for a vowel to be voiced and for a consonant to be voiceless, we consider the following physiological correlates: Given that the vocal tract is in position to produce a vowel, it is easier to produce a voiced vowel than a voiceless vowel. In the production of a vowel, the rush of air past the vocal chords tends to make them vibrate (compare with Bernoulli's Law), and it takes some effort to keep them from vibrating. In the production of a consonant, there is a constriction in the vocal tract, and any rush of air creates a back pressure, which tends to keep the vocal chords from vibrating. It takes an extra effort to force air through and cause vibration. Needless to say, all the physiological correlates for features have not been worked out and undoubtedly there are many features that are incorrectly or incompletely specified. Similarly, the notion

of markedness for phonological features is by no means entirely clear
or completely specified.

Since the facts about the ease of production of various speech
sounds are nowhere near complete, we must depend upon other evidence to provide clues as to which feature values are "normal," given
certain other values. We consider the following kinds of evidence:

1. *The earlier acquisition of the use of easier sounds.* Children
seem to acquire the ability to use easier sounds before the ability to
use harder ones. [See Remark C-1 and example (C-2) of Appendix C.
See also Jakobson, 1962.]

2. *The greater frequency of occurrence in phonological systems.*
Systematic phonemes corresponding to easy-to-produce speech sounds
seem to occur more frequently in the languages of the world than do
those that correspond to sounds that are hard to produce. Thus, it is
a rare language that does not have an /a/ or an /n/, and I have never
come across a language that did not have a /t/ (that is, a noncompact,
nongrave, voiceless stop consonant). Lateral fricatives, clicks,
rounded front vowels, and other relatively more difficult sounds occur
less frequently.

3. *The greater frequency of occurrence in individual languages.*
It seems to be the case that systematic phonemes corresponding to
relatively easy-to-produce sounds occur more frequently in the lexicon
of individual languages. For example, /j/, /o/, and /θ/ occur in fewer
English words than do /p/, /t/, or /k/. The principle of counting
marked phonological features, but not counting unmarked ones is
meant as a basis for the explanation of such phenomena.

4. *In phonological neutralization, the unmarked member of the
neutralized set of sounds is most likely to occur.* [See examples of
Remark C-1 and example (C-3) of Appendix C.]

When various empirical observations of this sort all seem to point to
the choice of a particular feature value in some environment as being
"normal" (unmarked), then we feel we have empirical support for
hypothesizing that that feature value is indeed unmarked.

R   C-3

Just as phonological features seem to be tied to the physiology of the
human vocal tract, so syntactic features seem to be tied to our conceptual system. Our notion of VERB seems to correspond in part to
the logical notion of "predicate"; nonstative verbs correspond in part
to activity predicates, while stative verbs correspond in part to property or state predicates. Thus, though the notion "normal" for syntactic features has no physiological basis, it is (as we shall see below)
a notion which is useful for explicating certain of our intuitions about
language and one which may eventually help us to understand what
the human conceptual apparatus is like.

We feel justified in extending the notions of "normal state" and
"markedness" directly from phonology since the same sort of em-

pirical evidence on which we base our conclusions about markedness in phonology seems to be present in syntax. For example:

1. Children seem to learn concrete nouns before they learn abstract ones; they seem to learn countable nouns before they learn uncountable ones; and so on. This would tend to make us hypothesize that −ABSTRACT and +COUNT, are the unmarked values of those features. We would then look for other evidence to confirm this.

2. and 3. Nonstative verbs and stative adjectives occur more frequently in the lexicons of individual languages than do stative verbs and nonstative adjectives.

4. In examples of syntactic neutralization, one feature value seems to turn up again and again wherever the given phenomenon occurs. This would tend to make us hypothesize that that value was the unmarked one. [For examples, see Section C.2 in Appendix C.]

R E-1

Note that Fodor and Katz permit disjunction in lexical items only if each branch of the disjunction has at least one semantic marker. Their lexical representation does not permit disjunctions of syntactic features.

R F-1

It has been brought to my attention by Robin Lakoff that sentences very similar to (F-30) may be interpreted in an entirely different way. Consider the sentences:

    a. Did they build the statue next to the courthouse?
    b. Did they build a statue next to the courthouse?

The only difference in these sentences is that b contains an indefinite article where a contains a definite article. Yet a assumes that some statue was built and asks about the location of it, while b asks whether a statue was built in a particular location. We have no idea how to account for this phenomenon.

R F-2

We are not arguing that there is *no* other way of accounting for the way in which negative and interrogative sentences containing adverbs are interpreted. It may very well be the case that one could find a number of extremely complex rules of semantic interpretation that would account for all the facts that we have brought forth so far and will bring forth in succeeding sections. That is, it may be that in order for us to maintain a simple rule for interpretation of all negative and interrogative sentences, we have to introduce complexities at least as great as those that we are trying to avoid. To present a *really* convincing case we would have to do more than argue that our handling of adverbs will account for the facts and that no one has yet found any other way of accounting for the facts. Rather we would have to show that *even if* someone were to come up with a complex set of rules for the interpretation of negative and interrogative sentences that contain adverbs, our adoption of such a set of rules would cause us to miss or to abandon certain generalities concerning a wide range of other phenomena. That is why the example of *I don't beat my wife because I like her* is a really crucial one. In order to account for the ambiguity of the sentence, one must assume that the negative element in it has two deep structure sources. (It is clear that neither of those sources can be within the S of *I like her,* since one can have the sentence *I don't beat my wife because she isn't ugly*—which has the same range of ambiguity and has a negative within the S following *because.*) Klima has pointed out a rather deep generalization about negative elements, namely, that only one negative element may occur per simple S in the deep structure. An overwhelming amount of syntactic evidence seems to favor this generalization [see Klima, 1964]. We can maintain this generalization only if we assume that reason adverbials come from higher S's. If, on the other hand, we were to assume that reason adverbials were introduced in some other fashion, say, as a constituent of the VP that immediately dominates the verb *beat,* then there would be one fewer S in the deep structures of sentences like (F-39) and, consequently, there would be more possible sources of negative elements than there would be deep structure S's. Therefore, if one asserts that reason adverbials do not come from "higher" simple sentences than the verbs that they modify, then one would have to abandon Klima's generalization that at most one negative element can occur per simple S in the deep structure of a sentence. It is in part to maintain such generalizations that we are proposing this analysis.

R   F-3

I assume that the internal structure of *because*-clauses is as given in the following illustrations:

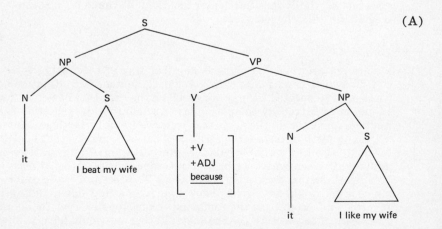

(A)

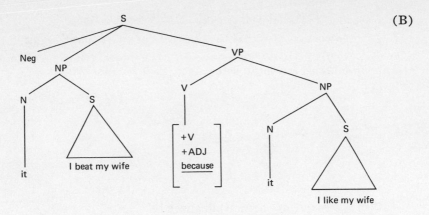

(A) and (B) correspond to (F-40') and (F-41'), respectively. After PREP-SPELLING [see Section A.1], we get (C) and (D).

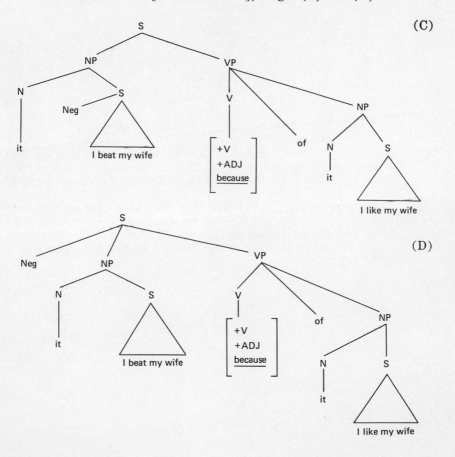

Note that if *it* is deleted, *of* will also be deleted, as in:

I am aware of it that he came → I am aware that he came   (E)

However, if the underlying structure of the object NP in (A) and (B) had contained a definite determiner, as in

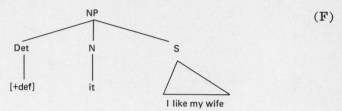

(F)

then *like* could have been nominalized to

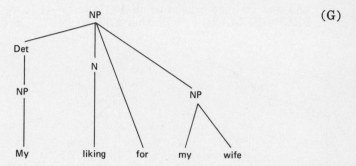

(G)

In this case, *of* would not drop and we would get *I don't beat my wife because* of *my liking for her*. (Recall that following prepositions are usually kept with adjectives, as in *I am aware* of *John's having shot Bill*.)

Actually, it may be the case that (A) and (B) are not deep structures at all, but are derived by FLIP. In that case, *because* can be thought of as having the lexical meaning of "result in" or "lead to." Thus, the deep structures of (A) and (B) may well be (H) and (I).

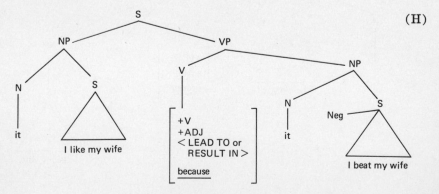

(H)

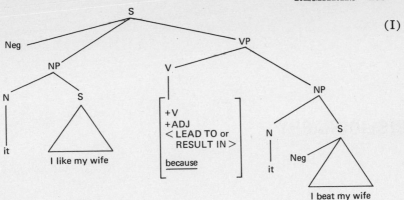

(I)

(H) would have the same meaning as *My liking for my wife leads to my not beating her*. (I), on the other hand, would have the same meaning as *My liking for my wife doesn't lead to my beating her*.

BIBLIOGRAPHY

Bennett, C. E. (1960). *New Latin Grammar*. New York: Allyn and Bacon.

Benveniste, E. (1946). "Structure des relations de personne dans le verbe." BSL, 43, pp. 1–12.

Bloomfield, L. (1933). *Language*. New York: Holt, Rinehart and Winston.

Chomsky, N. (1955). *The Logical Structure of Linguistic Theory*. Cambridge: M.I.T. Library. Mimeographed.

Chomsky, N. (1957). *Syntactic Structures*. The Hague: Mouton and Company.

Chomsky, N. (1962a). "A Transformational Approach to Syntax." In: A. A. Hill (Ed.). *Proceedings of the 1958 Conference on Problems of Linguistic Analysis in English*, pp. 124–148. Austin, Texas. Reprinted in Foder and Katz (1964).

Chomsky, N. (1962b). "Explanatory Models in Linguistics." In: E. Nagel, P. Suppes, A. Tarski (Eds.). *Logic, Methodology, and Philosophy of Science*. Stanford, California: Stanford University Press.

Chomsky, N. (1964). *Current Issues in Linguistic Theory*. The Hague: Mouton and Company. A slightly earlier version appears in Fodor and Katz (1964).

Chomsky, N. (1965a). "Topics in the Theory of Generative Grammar." In: T. A. Sebeok (Ed.). *Current Trends in Linguistics*, Vol. III. Linguistic Theory. The Hague: Mouton and Company.

Chomsky, N. (1965b). *Aspects of the Theory of Syntax*. Cambridge: The M.I.T. Press.

Chomsky, N., and M. Halle (1968). *The Sound Pattern of English*. New York: Harper and Row.

Fodor, J. A., and J. J. Katz (Eds.). (1964). *The Structure of Language: Readings in the Philosophy of Language*. Englewood Cliffs, N.J.: Prentice-Hall.

Fraser, J. B. (1965). *An Examination of the Verb-Particle Construction in English*. Unpublished doctoral dissertation, Cambridge, M.I.T.

Hall, B. (1965). *Subject and Object in English*. Unpublished doctoral dissertation, Cambridge, M.I.T.

Harris, Z. (1964). "Discourse Analysis." In: Fodor and Katz (1964). Originally appeared in *Language*, 28, pp. 1–30.

Jakobson, R. (1962). "Kindersprache, Aphasie, und Allgemeine Lautgesetre." *Selected Writings*, I. The Hague: Mouton and Company.

Jespersen, O. (1909–1949). *A Modern English Grammar*, seven volumes. London: Allen and Unwin.

Katz, J. J., and P. Postal (1964). *An Integrated Theory of Linguistic Descriptions*. Cambridge: The M.I.T. Press.

Klima, E. (1964). "Negation in English." In: Fodor and Katz (1964).

Lees, R. B. (1960a). *The Grammar of English Nominalizations*. The Hague: Mouton and Company.

Lees, R. B. (1960b). "A Multiply Ambiguous Adjectival Construction in English." *Language*, 36, pp. 207–221.

Lees, R. B. (1961). "Grammatical Analysis of the English Comparative Construction." *Word*, 17, pp. 171–185.

Mitre Corporation. *English Preprocessor Manual*. Information System Language Studies No. 7, SR-132. Bedford, Massachusetts: Mitre Corporation.

Postal, P. M. (1964a). *Constituent Structure: A Study of Contemporary Models of Syntactic Description*. The Hague: Mouton and Company.

Postal, P. M. (1964b). "Underlying and Superficial Linguistic Structure." *Harvard Educational Review*, 34, pp. 246–266.

Postal, P. M. (1964c). "Limitations of Phrase Structure Grammars." In: Fodor and Katz (1964).

Rosenbaum, P. S. (1967). *The Grammar of English Predicate Complement Constructions*. Cambridge: The M.I.T. Press.